KUUSH-NUBA

AMURUGAN BAHYETE

BALBOA.
PRESS
A DIVISION OF HAY HOUSE

Balboa Press books may be ordered through booksellers or by contacting:

Balboa Press
A Division of Hay House
1663 Liberty Drive
Bloomington, IN 47403
www.balboapress.com
1 (877) 407-4847

ISBN: 978-1-5043-9486-4 (sc)
ISBN: 978-1-5043-9487-1 (e)

Print information available on the last page.

Balboa Press rev. date: 01/05/2018

Contents

Ookan...1

Eeji..7

Eeta..12

Eeri..15

Aarun..19

Eeta..23

Umina Saba Nubian..29

Eejo..42

Eesan..48

Eewaa...52

Dismal Swamp..58

San Basilio...61

Maluala..64

Characteristics..69

Appendix...71

Glossary..73

NtuNyeye..75

Commercial Break...81

OOKAN

The greatest civilization can attest that nothing is more fundamental than- **know thyself**. How can one move in the external world without the internal being (at one *atone*ment) of your existence. The promise of creation is to escalate forthrightly while compulsory; and for what the universe needs from each of us is to stay in accordance with our personal destiny. You have been given a soul to complete a mission and also to ascend, remove personal karmic impurities and to recognize, **a truer Source** and also of those things within yourself. Then as to recognize a higher being of and in oneself is the most divine return to **our** Source beyond time and theorems. When matter and existence disappear all that is left and will remain is *spirit* and soul. But within the law of complimentary opposites is the most prudent judicious question for any human being to analyze; and that is to excavate the formulation of the collective in being one with the universe. A person must know who she or he is in relation to how they are interrelated to everything else in the universe so that also she or he will or *sees it*; with a shared experience of the many. This sharing includes going along our travels crossing numerous living entities. They meaning those experiences are inclusive with purpose and reason within us; and that our separate discoveries are not withholding tribulations as they are sections of a lifelong quest. This inescapable and higher will can never cease; for it is eternity which sheds time which will involve truth and love and wisdom for you. What one can *do* and see in anything is included in everything; and everything comes from the Source of truth.

The question is what strengthens the spirit and what sustains it; and to acquiesce with unselfishness by such issues of love/wisdom/truth knowingly displayed with all. The next step is to proceed *within* and in your daily life to yield to a personal realization. You can not judge others, which is not a good characteristic, until coming to the ultimate correct judgment of yourself; and even at that moment one should not judge or act upon it. That is a maturation and actualization that can take a while but it shall arrive about by the proper faculties. Those would include *meditation→experience→elders→critical advice→introspection→ humility* and as to bring about something fully comprehensive to encompass our personal destiny and goals. A nation needs people who have a foundation. We have to cement each other and one another on an unwavering platform of heritage and keep our truth and culture vigorously sturdy **as our remedy**; before attempting other endeavors of nationalistic imperativeness.

But we are focusing on you, family, community, and collective. This will lead to all the greater prospects and probabilities and perspectives of yourself. The actual definition of yourself does not need an explanation (everything is 360 degrees) still we arrive at that which is hardest to know; and sometimes our toughest answer to get to is **merely** your reality and you. We think we may know who we are but we have to **purely reach out** and absorb erudition that each breath has granted us. Therefore as easy as it is to have recognition, being complimentarily opposite, it may still become hardest in its attainment. *What we thought of as the easiest question sometimes comes back to the apogee* *of the circle as the most difficult.* That realization is not answered by oneself but by the collective effort. *We will get there after while soon enough- together.*

Family is a group of individuals who you have blood relations with; along to numbering a very few to a very many (depending on the person) and your obligations are there because they have been there since the beginning of your inception or conception. Those who you feel close to and who have your concerns *and* are genuinely thoughtful of your considerations also are what we are going to call, with a similar holistic mindset, your spiritual family group. Community are those who you live among and must see everyday and therefore you should have a respect for them as to include nature/trees/spirits/animals from the breathing of the same air; being in the same vicinity. Collective is a step wider or ahead of nation or a collection of nations meaning all of us as Afrikan people **those who started humanity;** in matters of all of the sciences including culture. We are the record that everybody keeps sampling and playing on the worldwide radio of heritage, quite obvious. These others and people have been given love from us and sometimes without giving us adequate recognition; and these global cultural reforms which we have given to the world has since then evolved into a very distinct and cultural everyday usage in the daily patterns of the many lives on this planet having become globally critical. We are the proven gateway to all sciences and arts that allow others to use what we explored millions of years before their existence; to continue along with new titivations. It started with our culture and heritage deep in the heart of Africa and that spread throughout the world. That word heritage is more fitting and will replace history in our deliberations and inclinations. We will also use cultural heritage instead of race because this is not a competition; to outdo another suite of human beings because we are here together. *This mindset will help bring us more love and answers.*

We are going to need everything to get to anything (realistically as a team). But to love yourself; you have to know yourself honestly, your deficiencies and edicts. You have been sent here with each of us; and have emerged along with your **soul** to unquestionably materialize to this dimension with a quest to fulfill that love and purpose. But **That** is found in ourselves. But how do we get to that and therefore there- find out.

It does not matter whether you are broken as long as you have become settled with those issues and work towards solving them because (life is a long process of expiation with pain and joy to reflect a removal of impurities) to realize this as a part of the situation is necessary; and of the circumstances/parents/life you have chosen in the spirit realm. We have now arrived to the keys of consciousness. You always have the final say *even in spirit*; and **before arriving** to craft your path to actuality it shall become settled with determination. This is getting deeper to what others do not want you to know; which is how to control your **soul**. You have the answers to every one of your questions and are complete in everything you need; already given to each and every one of us from **Source** in the body's template of our many cells. That does not need any embellishment and merely just means we are never without Source and never far away from the aim of **our** goals. But it is our solution. But even if some are contemptuously having refusal to see that truth in the light from higher and lower experiences blessed upon from a greater ordained entity, then you have lost your soul. Conversely, with family and nation you and the team can find it again. You must return to the mission intended; and that is decoded for you being accurately situated in the stars and galaxy. The law of complimentary opposites says helping me is helping yourself. The resolution and ripostes are with Source and within us to find everything around our being thoroughly for an answer; and in utilizing all that is within and outside of us evolving in our lives. Each of us should assist our sister or brother along as we toil to get there; for we are all connected. This is on an individual basis surely. But also as part of a law regardless that we are together and that remains true and forever. This is in our universe's 360 degrees of interpretation as to never have to sustain without the interconnection of our fellow woman or man.

That means that the many is made of One and Source and that one can drive past the barriers because of the many parts. You did not wake up *alone* even when sitting in the most reclusive space because alone is only recognizing yourself with Source and the unity within yourself to manufacture something far greater for the rest of humanity. The self is the integration of the many parts of the universe. Yes, our goal is that we are going to integrate with the widespread congregation of family and community and collective. But with taking a step backwards it is not problematic for it is only to maybe take three steps forward ultimately *in what resides in your intuition*; which is what has inclined you to make a statement on this journey- your life.

That is a hard question, what to do while you are here, then to answer that correctly is only for you to answer; and conversely you do not have to do it alone but it must initially start with oneself. What makes you feel good and is part of your personality is from the holy feat of giving joy to **you**; to accomplish and spread and match each and every one us. That is a synergy with others in furthering the love of spirit/family/community/nation. It is clarifying the natural way of what others see in you as a reciprocal talent and appeasement; that is subsequently taken and utilized by **our** people. It is our greatest need for you to see this; and meet and summon up to your godly level. But this does not mean it will not become hard and that it is not work. The difficulty of responsibility is *to see* the joy of work for the greater benefit. Life is not always going to have you do what you want; but you should as much as possible (90% of your breathing) mystically remain happy. That is where love and community and nation arrive in the resin of your thoughts. You are doing this for us and **them,** unknown kinfolk and unborn spirits, as we are the love of a nation.

This can appear from a lot of meditation and in searching from the many god- given talents that you possess and were bestowed. *But what is the best way to put them to use.* We all have something to give as a piece of the pie. *Then still your self may need direction.*

I told you life is not meant for one to exist- alone. The family can provide answers. The community can provide solutions. Our nation can deter untruths and lead to the right bearing. Then you will arrive at the *spirit* of yourself; and know what is ample in the victory of life.

The family began our list. It is going to show you *your first mirror and echo back some truths to your personality* (which in reality is the shaping of a pathway along with purpose) providing your culture, diet, pedagogy, axiology, heritage, spirituality, and locution. This is the first drawing board and receptacle of your actions. *It is* stated once again that family is not always blood- related; rather those later on in your life who in particular have nurtured and cultivated you from a tiny plant to an enormous sequoia in making everyone proud.

Our family and **our way** of family is going to teach you values; and sometimes hurt your feelings to make you stronger. But righteously it has love there, in those actions. We have to take critical examination and critique to get to higher places. Your family is to cleanse as much as possible the rough edges of what you may encounter tomorrow at a mature or young age; and you are to surely take those findings with you *to stick with* you. They should build you up more than they bring you down. These people are here to smite raw gold into jewelry. That is implementing the purity of our family/ communal/national steadfastness with your strengths as you conquer and snake and overcome your weaknesses in the daily trudge of living. They see your best attributes and traits; and characteristics

to tell you how to use each and every one of them for the future. It is a process that should have the maintenance of discipline and teaching; inclusive also of your steps towards learning and forward progression.

The community is to *appraise and inspect* this masterpiece because you are and still are the next extension of them. They are going to give their word and words in what they have seen all along, respectful and considerate of needed advice. They are the proofreaders of your thesis and proposal which has been meticulously edited by our prior step- family. These individuals are not always correct and are not to overstep their bounds because you and family should know yourself better than anyone. But we need to look at information from an enterprising totality of angles. **You might have to search from more than just what is being given from them…but the love is there**.

This is going to bring you undoubtedly to self. The *spirit* and **soul** are in tuned for being one together from/with the many that we have mentioned earlier; as in constructing the product of you. That is using our world and surroundings in attempting to define the result of you; and of trying to find purpose. The most obvious first community is family. *Then the family and community are going to help you exhibit the necessities of criteria in your standard assertion to the universe of what makes correspondence to Source (returning to your answer of self appraisal/recognition/opulence) as the goal of everyone is to become a god- like deity while being mortal.* But we must first fuse what Source has given; as with the best of you to make this decision.

We have gone to community but let's go to the mountain of it- the elders. They are here with profound insight and direction. They are here to see what is best for the whole. They may see or have seen the talent and zeal that you have; which they may have had at one time in themselves. But their final reclamation in life on this journey is to intermingle as a stepping stone the facilitating of your greatness with those greater characteristics.

That is why we listen to our elders and give praise to them and to spirits. They hope to partake in the vision, even if they are not here physically, smiling heavenly when the achievement is done for the fulfillment of community. They know they can not leave behind anything that will hinder community and want you to seek them. They have many answers as they prepare to answer the unknown and unfathomable. *We will consign there with them one day.* Their affects of wisdom have been bequeathed to us forever as they are ubiquitously and perennially here as **shrines of knowledge** for us to gather as they shape our lives. These people (spirits) give us what we need to find in ourselves and clearly affirm what are some of the best potentialities of ourselves.

Our Ancestors have researched and exalted and traversed for the answers to many questions which took the accumulation and the expertise of generations being passed down to the level of our present-day condition. They have seen times and struggle they wish for us not to endure or retrospect. They know and **truly know** the meaning of sacrifice. When and how are we going to get there without truly *knowing* them.

Those are Ancestors of thousands of years ago to those close to the family's past and those which we have touched like grandparents; and to those who are still around who can proffer assistance. We have to know their lives and guidance are immeasurable. Their restitution is of priceless- value. But you have to get to them and engage with them before some of the detriments of old age keep them from giving you their best. **Some have given of themselves and relinquished their desires for others to have a chance**.

The scholars and laborers who have lived prior to our coming to earth need holy recognition and gratitude as *we travel* the roads they have paved. That means going to see the pyramids to the wonders we have built around the world and to visiting family and the local graves because we must give honor **to this**. But the way to accomplish this task basically outside of ritual is to live with honor. That is knowing yourself and handling destiny. I and nation hope we can do this, projecting reverence.

When we have listened to our mind and our elders and our hearts so that no one can compete with us then we as a group of individuals eradicate divisiveness and will embody a *unified spiritual* nation. We as individuals and a people are to reshape and change the world of existence. **Our talents are too rich to hold in one house**. You will become cluttered and suffocate yourself. *That is what happens when you do not find yourself but lean toward directives not in your forecast or not of your specific responsibility; and that wandering is ill stricken which will get you lost.* Each of us has been given a hammer of talents and a nail of responsibility to secure, in rebuilding the house of our people and culture. We brought civilization to the world once, and partly because of the fall of our digressive negligence, we are going to have to do it again as the progenitors of the sunrise. We need you to find yourself and to stretch **and to reach to** us simply because our circle is not complete without holding your hand. That is to say use life as a tool of your ascension. The light will appear once you get to know who you are; and by those actions get deemed worthy of our nascent approbation. Your responsibility is to incorporate in your heart and soul the blocks that will level us to return forward (not bring us back) to the immanent truth.

THE ENTIRITY OF YOU IS MOLDED AND FILTERED for THE BEST OF THE INDIVIDUAL BY THE WHOLE

EEJI

But is this our culture or has it been made our culture. **We** have to define what is best for us and should only offer the solutions/culture/programs that are for our unanimity. How can you live oppressed and *still believe* in freedom. We are the answers; in our interactions for expanding with each other. But the answer is permanently believing and sustaining for each other, in keeping our spirit alive to enlighten once more- perpetually, AMUN.

It is truly imperative to live as we want to live as an **Afrikan** nation and culture and a people defined. Nation is earnestly not confined to any preposterous boundaries and is the recognizing, as we are **Afrikan**, of groups of solidified individuals contributing to a collective mindset. It is similar to people being part of steeler nation or Hokie nation which could stretch anywhere. But are you pulling for the same team or living with the oppression mentality. Where have you been that expresses your culture (most of which optimistically is at home) if you even know what is **real culture** as it pertains to you. But *this is as necessary* as breathing in doing all of the things a human being needs to do in her or his best interests. Where is the opportunity to chase our interpretations to become fully addressed and heard on a level that melts for us; and with us into this society. We have to stand on **our** nationalistic own to have progression.

You have to get up with urgency. We had reformed and maladapted in slavery for base typical survival. That is inclusive too of imperialism and colonialism and the bequeathing of more recent findings in the detriments of our accustoming into the present culture which is of a jointly lethal psychological make- up. What do we alter, what do we use as good, and **what** needs complete upheaval. This is needed in the journey of finding yourself and to place something here before making ascension.

This is not who we are as the heritage and cultural pride of our Ancestors' past; or really of our recent own accomplishments which resonate profoundly **who we are** just as will so much more when we realize it. But who has led to the continuity and resurgence of all entertainment and arts other than the blood of Itopians and the Afrikan (including most certainly culture others have staked as theirs such as philosophy not from greeks to montu which is the oldest form of martial arts not from Asiatic sources to the building of ships also chariots which first came from Kemet) not to mention the exacting academics from chemistry of the body to anything dealing with the stars. It seems everyone has a stake in these bakra lies to help destroy us. People take from us as if it was their right because we have not reestablished a culture *from the many cultures that* we have created with unyielding togetherness; hopefully being premiere to the **Afrikan** and not for everyone else to have stockade. This is for the individual and the community and for **our** nation in realizing, to take at this moment, the recognition and responsible acceptance in supplying the tools we need for distinction not extinction. We have had our science and ingenuity taken away from us for market value leading to consumerism reverting us back to the creative *drawing board*. We are **the most creative people on earth because we started humanity and womankind and are sometimes forced too often to use that natural inclination, as it becomes detrimental to our efforts**. We are thinking of so many things for America from music to slang to clothing that it takes away from our prosperity and focus and direction on more important matters. This is the same uniqueness and energy as a nation we could use to reapplying our sciences; rather than providing each and every other racial backgrounds a financial opportunity for covetously devouring our community. That style/swag everyone tries to imitate is the same waste of time and low level measurement we at times emphasize, instead of measuring ourselves with accomplishments of culture and science that could seize the impending world, which our people usually give more money to without receiving a dime back to get ahead among the franchising global neighborhood. Then the same bakra sells and tells among anyone who has a dollar of how to manufacture their pecuniary interest; to devilishly redistribute our same progeny and then to dictate how we should act as true Africans or African- Americans.

That is why this is not our culture. *Who can hear me really*. It is simple and easy that we must convey to our people what we have determined as vital to us in to vivaciously instilling personal/community/galactic information; for needed truth at last, in our final step. Then with this we will show how it should evidently filter in with being part of the process of relaying it among our youth and greatest contemporaries. That is the true love of **ourselves** just dealing just with us. We can generally do anything. We have to benefit from every scarce commodity and congruous spiritual additive of **our** culture whether intangible or tangible, rehabilitating commercialized marketing ploys, to make a way for other generations to unlock the door in our inexorable progression to newer thoughts and making it modern for our utilization as a singular **Afrikan** people. When this prepared scheme to converge us is annexed by not relating to entertainment mechanisms which divert us from the mighty flow of the river concerning science and mathematical inquiry (the barrage is ignited) for it is **our** adolescents which have the minds of major constructive relevance; that will cross all restrictions to the higher state, hopefully in augmenting the building of a nation.

But we have to return forward to **our** cultural pedestal which is naturally the summit of truth and axiological living. We are axiomatic souls that occupy bodies for our journeys; and while helping all, each of us are still at the same time developing our own **soul**. But why is it that we have the greatest shoulders to stand on but still can not get off of the ground. It is maybe because we are taking our heritage from the enemy and walking by in life too immensely focused on minuscule meager garbage (materialism- sports-

religion- financial predicaments- wrong diet- hellidays- violence- selfish overconsuming- love) to not have time to glimpse that our wings stretch to heaven and afar. This external world has some bakra bastard telling you what is precise and reasonable and is falsely shaping our culture.

We are searching for the abyss to cement the change in our situation in adhering to our eternity. That deep evermore is found in a book or talking to elders or researching *to find us* palpably returning development forward to the peak- apex **OUR MASTER CREATOR**. We have *to remove the sordid defects and muds that have been institutionalized and given to us by a different people* **not ourselves**. You have to make what is right exactly that, what is right.

It is a simple decision to digress or have progression by having the courage/freedom/toughness/resiliency to break away from the normality of such an establishment to set the truth for **our**selves and to not mislead our watoto(Afrikan babies) by moving ahead. When are you going to read a book to explain to the children the rites and immense sovereigns of who we are- **The Afrikan**. Then keep reading because it is the duty of our **Afrikan** *unsurpassed heritage* and of the infinite vast information (that one person could never engulf in a hundred years of work to retell) to make sure the factual truth is not disintegrated and forgotten; **which is why we need cooperative education** from community. We need to do this by taking from the past to incorporate the nation's future to what is the present, our gift.

You have to look towards and forwards to the future and work on the present. That is to say we **must look** to ourselves and stay looking that way. You can become adroit and return to the moment and stay prescient. We have stated that love of self is the highest existence and being. But we can not have that without the honest reflection of who we are and cultural recognition.

This is a job (accomplishment) which needs **our** support. That means looking at our people with the toughest reflecting mirror. It is unacceptable for anyone to tell us *anything* ranging from political to social to ancient past about **who we are**; and no one should even think to know more of our condition than we do in the least instance. We have just already stated that it is needed to do the research and to teach yourself; and absolve the predicament for having a solution with the unbounded honor/sophistication/valor of still teaching our children. But honestly, in referring to heritage, when we talk of the bad it is yet more beautiful for us because as a true reflection of learning from our mistakes it shows and bares the perseverance which has made us much better and even stronger. These are the lessons we have learned from the Ancestors in their existence.

We need cultural recognition. We need **our** heritage put in our words, more in a later chapter. That is the only way to overcome and *see that we will rise again*. But with the correct knowledge and purpose we have to put the right thoughts into action.

The task or issue of cultural reform is to return us to the most powerful people in the world. Our antecedents have the longest history. It is an effort of knowing the facts with *assiduous application* to **our** people for self. That will revert continuously forward to the big *Community Nation Universe*, constantly giving yourself growth and erudition. We shall spread our reality and truth; and to acquire the truth of heritage.

But all of us have to do the work. We need people with enthusiasm in what they are learning about in our heritage to go to the deepest bottoms in retrieving data and dispatching it with an alacritous teaching style to instill pride. That fervor and fever is the best contagious stroke to have been diagnosed from; and is needed by our people. That is the process of having an individual fort or base to operate from in knowledge of self, to what best fits you to study and share forward to the nation. We have to have this for the babies who are coming to rule the world. **The love of what is accurate and what we do not know and what we should come to know is love**. I hope you *see* my overstanding and purpose.

Our cultures and undoubtedly proud heritage are the foundation of the world and its wisdom. Our cultural similarities within other ethnic groups and illustrious heritages which have and are still notably spanning the planet; peak also to illustrate the immensity of **our** regal importance and the many stylistic shared techniques that can coalesce and keeps rising along with those cross- overs which should bring us more emphatically together. The very Essence is waiting on us for the Inception to further our people to destiny and out of proclaimed misery. Our grabbing on to and taking hold of such; and conceptualizing the truth **in such** profoundness is the only thing that is *getting us ready*.

But everyone is needed in keeping us to gather such perspective and of knowing what shall happen from our returned greatness.

We are to return to goddesses and gods, stated as fact. That is the truth that can not and is not seen under a microscope. Well that is unless you are talking about melanin- uncompromised godliness. That is away from any unbelieving or linear perspective. You do not have to take it from me but in meditation take it from yourself and get to that level. We were categorically there before and on deck *to get there* again.

It is our recognition of heritage that will allow us to eliminate false truths that pollute the minds of **our** future. We are not to debate with idiots what is our heritage and truth of antiquity but solely teach it to our children. Then we have to have the children restructure themselves, suns of light, from the bombing of misinformation that is to disenfranchise us **as a** global nation. We have once civilized and given heritage and culture to this planet thus needing in having again to truly reaffirm to this world; then why is someone giving it back to us when we need to reconstruct and lead them into the light of destiny. The people will have richness with a dissident reality and a mathematical and scientific genius solidified in the cultural renewal of each and every **Afrikan** for everyone (as of today). We can use our luxurious historians/poets/scientists/musicians/doctors. We can say things in Nubian and Yoruba and Twi while giving immense amplification to their full meaning. That is surely how we are going to carry restoration and re- calibrate vibration. Then we will notice we have so much in common that is interchangeable and not baffling to our perplexities of grand supplementation. It is everything that is **our thing**. Persistently, we rummage to gather our data and become diligent and return to it. The answers we shall get to is a single source of information which is Africa from Lake Mwanza Nyanza to KMT to Dravidian Kushitic India.

TRUTH IS a LIGHT THAT DOES NOT CAST A SHADOW

EETA

It is simple; and the question is what and when are you going to put community ahead of your selfish wants/desires/egoism. What can you do to do that; that is when things are better for us. But the trick has been for as close to any eternity in dealing *with our lower self,* is to see visibly everything as a whole and connected. The lower self feeds this world from multitudes of static variations and vibrations. But to the masses it is a flavorsome unhealthy meal tastefully appeasing for one to prefer to have things out of context

(getting away from the nutrition of your soul or what your body needs to have) not giving what is proper to nourish **the temple**. When you have an excuse for validating malignant acts it is just measly conciliation and cloaking satisfaction with purity; which is false. But we know it truly does work better when you have a meaningful defined living; and not with the previously mentioned way. What is it that is best for us is sometimes hard to gulp down; and the uneasiness that comes with that is a *temporary provision* of love and order.

The agitating soreness escapes after a workout becomes regular with time and the bland food of a healthy diet becomes appetizing; and the awkwardness of relationships become amicable with familiarity. When you think otherwise that life is precious and without obstacles then we know that truly is a mistake, at the same time inhibiting to yourself. We go through pain to get into delight. The harboring of any weakness is that of leaving and of dropping off pain to get to a newer height and stronger. But the pain is only a mental condition *of un- acceptance.*

The grief of a family member is gone when you know she or he are in a more surpassed place. You have to give up something for the Sunnum Bunnom to have anything. That is sometimes giving up the devious things which is to some what is called life, to have bliss. It takes due introspection and a strategic sacrificial will; that is to carry out the course

(pun intended with coarse) of adversity and necessities. **You have to offer your hand**. That is the quality which is needed and raised in anyone or any solitary/solidified group who has the proclivity to start a nation. The preceding chapters gave direction and advancement in and with inner- sight. That being of the love and insight of what you have to offer, you have to take action. But you now have to live up to those works and wants. **We have to want it together** and immediately. These are the words said internally to yourself to recuperate and to take your first step; to the love of a nation and the community for perfection. When you do not have altruism or sacrifice or determination we will falter to an undue end; when we only needed collaboration.

That lack of support and teamwork is the scratch which becomes a crack in the collective foundation, as things amplify, from diminutive onsets. Then these become huge problems. How can we have this when we can overcome them. Well in keeping aware and definite of the damaging situation you just may have to have the strength to sacrifice something of your own.

You and we or us do not have a dilemma when there is a collective balance of everyone doing their part. We all are giving something for the greater beneficial continuity. But even if when doing so make sure it does not unfavorably eradicate something of your **soul** or of self along with not to falter the family/community/collective. Those are the forerunners and unquestionably the foundation of our purpose.

Why should you have to give up so much or focus on others who are negligent of themselves (we want spiritual catalyst and movers) not those with judgment because everyone is not awakened at the same time. We do not want you to give up everything; and that is why others are needed to restore their direction with their timeliness from looking at your example and virtuosity. It will occur in time. But during that time and meanwhile just focus on what you can accomplish regardless of what you must forgo without killing the future of those who depend on you most each day foregone and presently.

We and you should want to assist future generations who look just like you. We have to have confidence in knowing who we are and the cultural reform of being able to involve others later; and having eventually **realized** victorious attainment. Where is your sisterhood/brotherhood/unanimity and caring nature and do you offer it. Well plainly stated this is offering to tell you we need it. But we do not want valid reasons more accurately termed excuses; when appearing to handle what is paramount for the whole rather than the single individual. We do not want you to give false reasons as to why things should work out better *only advantageous to a few* and yourself in this way. We do not, keeping a fruitful balance, want or should become burdening to separate woman or man from what is principal to them in life. But we do want **our** goal attained. You might have to take some time to grow before you can offer your righteous assistance. Then again you may have to have an expedition to prevail; to return home a more complete being or woman or man. You have to use good sense. That is to say if we endanger any community or family or relationship then we have lost a sense of the prowess of building a nation. You can have a benevolent subsistence with all of us without demanding any attention *to selfish* tautological problems; and then from glory onwards want to make it to the point where we can altogether stand firmly.

BUT KEY TO FINDING YOUR GOAL IS TO STUDY AND ASK QUESTIONS OF ELDERS AND OF MEDITATION

EERI

When you are giving someone or anyone anything to learn you should better have your stuff together. A person is not required in being the overpowering best hunter when passing on the skills, to offspring or the next generation, just necessary in of being a competent hunter. It is knowing why and how to fit your better proficiency (expertise of finding what to teach). Your promotion and willingness of facilitating the correct substantial content matters undoubtedly most in being- more relevant. But it is learning **how to learn before** taking the privilege and functions of teaching what others should learn from your endeavors/thoughts/experiences in life. We just want for the children the lessons imparted in the right way.

You can not think you know it all or have everything solved because Source will create/expand/produce a million more questions. This transmitted within a blinking of an eye beyond your human finite comprehension. Greatly attributing, it is about constant renewal. It is subsisting to master all that you can while on earth and share it with others (finding knowledge of self) happiness and self- destination. You are taking along with this *spirit* and with the **soul** your actions which are cumulatively distinctive. This is especially for your internal alchemy; with venturing to attempt the use of all personal experience as growth. But this takes control and elevation.

It takes substantial pious devotion to have balance and discipline and harmony. You can do that- it. One can master many things. That is something for your ideals. No one is going to have complete mastery of all conceptualizations because we have not *reemerged or fused our existence* forward to Source; transitioned to being called a higher power.

But once again we can get there. We need you to know that and what it is that you can engender best; and for you to have found that in yourself. That is part of your destiny and generosity to the nation. Each step and second is commanding in your experience of life; in providing the next step or birth, some call death, of being born again to something greater. That is an **essentially higher** wedding. But life has a strategic- cosmic format. The universe ostentatiously is a complete mental forthcoming and the key eternally is knowing that.

That should take us to a level or status higher than others; which is of a vivacious expert authenticity, to raise the agenda of preserving our nation. That we are serious should not take nor require exclamatory phrases or elaboration. We just need to get the job done. Then and maybe first we need to do the job, expertly.

But what are you going to offer or have as your input. We and each and every person **should/ needs** to have something to teach obviously for the youth. Our brightest smiles are seeing theirs and realizing we have made a correct decision for the *future*. Then we have put towards the future properly for the reasons of to coerce and to synergize; and towards the right path. The vocation is completed upon that goal.

You can sometimes eat the fruit even after your expiration or having transitioned. We just want to see the work completed because our Ancestors were sagacious in taking time over generations to accomplish a goal wanting not to have better for themselves but for those who will follow them. That is them *and us*. When you do a good deed in life **good deeds** will *roll over in the spiritual realm* for you; and having brought them about while leading to something positive without always having immediate response is not for you to decide but to carry on lovingly. Everyone is not going to have the ability in witnessing the fruition from **our** goal. But that person does not worry leaving this earth without partaking of the finished product for it was her or his time to having answered Source the Great Mystery or summit. That is because maybe returning later in tasting the sweet joy of this accomplishment to exist by the cycle of birth and rebirth. Then eventually receiving unto herself or himself. We can not and will not escape from the Great Cosmic- Law. That is why **we** must teach the babies because they are the ones who are maybe teaching you one day; for this is incarnating the goddess and godliness of ourselves which brings about change in the affirmative direction.

The lesson clearly, without mere hesitation, is that it is giving which makes life worth it. Our dexterity and persuasive affluence should handle that matter. It should not take much but cooperative effort if we are a mindful and spiritual people. **When are we going to work together** beyond all lines that have been obstructing our top of the mountaintop; and that someone has set for us. It is the time for us to meander apart from those imperatives which are pertaining to our diversity and cultural unity.

We do not need that divisiveness **to have us and our best**. But let's get forward to the point of what is the personal best of you in offering what you can make under the right environs and not being selfish. We can not have what is selfish to exist (your vanity or disillusioned ego) for sometimes what you love most to do is not what you are best at; and we need **your best** to grow. The past and present circumstances *are obliging* and are in your partiality of being of a more profound vastness because of you; we as a collective are always looking for direct/future/patient/substantial improvement. This far too critically has the most application with children, crisis management, family, and community.

One must remember that nation starts with being real with yourself and cognizant and truthful with those around you. But we must find a craft for the endogenous spark, coruscation of your attributes, the verdict of within. That external community and support will help guide us; which also gives and extends to character. We have to have such a set of mind. We have to find what is best for each of us as individuals to teach; and our assessment of communal resources.

But interestingly enough this text also shows how each lesson is intermingled as is in life for the cumulative wholesome overstanding. We do not need an internecine delay because the ready and open- eyed public can stray to something destructive by wasting time and not comprehensively observing the exigency. That is to say find out what you do best because we need to stay constructive. The more each jiffy goes by the more easily it is for our idle and adolescent minds to succumb to the distractions set forth by the enemy to impend failure.

Once stated and once again you are not required in being the Magic Johnson or Willie Mays of whatever field just recommended high level work- good effort. You have to have the ability to convey in an unambiguous approach what you have learned. I hope I am doing that, taking my own lesson, to teach and persuade and communicate some of my findings. That is a simplistic and an easy group effort for teachers and students when the community is involved. But if you do not know what you are talking about then stop telling people what or how to do it; *when you do not know it* yourself.

This goes to all aspects from crafts in retelling myth to physical work or **the heritage** of explaining any of our academia. We expand further than all people from what has been laid before us and are higher than any other by us having done things simply thousands and millions of years ago (mathematics science astronomy etiology). *But we can easily maintain those acute edicts because they have been set before us in the proper sequence.* Everything happens for a reason and nothing is by chance, we have **gone through certain** things to arrive at certain places, know this and distinguish it in your life. We have been in many troubles in our heritage; and the love of continuing forward was accompanied by a teaching from an elder or someone gratefully not being stationary in our life for to later possess the uncovering of our direction in the light. This vow or oath is ensuring hopelessly to endure that capsizing lineage of our natural superiority.

THE LESSONS HAVE to STAY OPEN TO RENDITIONS AND INNOVATIONS AS LONG AS EACH PREMISE REMAINS SIMILAR FOR THE CORE EFFECT

AARUN

You have to pray to your own goddesses and gods and in the most comfortable way of your own power. Why take on gods not of your own culture; and who do not look like you while being part of the digression in an encumbering situation to your fulfillment. That is bullshit without question; or any spiritual practice which does not make way for personal innovation and reformation. **That is a necessity to allow your love expressed in your way.** Religion is a groupthink process different from sacred religion, which knows Source is ever- forming with change, in allowing personal expression. This is for you and the adherents to discover their own path while keeping with the tenets of the ideology without being burdened to conformity. No one can get **there** but yourself to the unquestionable truthful meaning of why you were given a soul and a personal journey.

Your belief in Source is key to the brood and function of a nation. The oppressor can not oppress a spiritually cohesive people with strength in their eschatology. This makes a people or nation or battalion a culturally binding people. Those *are blessed* who are mutually gender respectful with corollary reverence to Source and show profound regard to the elderly or aged. The proud heritage instilled by ourselves from ancient tested and proven ways is the cornerstone in reckoning for us as a people with victory against a people who are devious and hope to never succumb; but we fear not those who are inferior and who wish for our destruction. **But who art lost art thou who can not define their own goddess and god worship.**

It is virtually impossible by any means of **heritage** to continue without having the facts and the light told from our enlightened mouths of those who have risen themselves fully. They are **our** elders/ warriors/priesthood/scholars. But cowardly opposition is determined to have our directive cut; for one of the chief weapons in this fight is that the enemy will march forward unless confronted. Then and there it is evident we must fight soulfully along with mentally; and knowing that we will die upright gaining a first far more respect than to have them *shackle our souls*. The fight once you have found yourself is for you to have intact that steadiness of your soul completely; and spiritual and cultural nature. You are *on the road to who you are* in the eyes of community and Source and the collective.

You are starting to remove the dross to what is a preeminent fit; and to a greater contribution to your family and nation, as you are gold in the purifying **earthly** fire. That is living everyday to become *exponentially better*. This *is onerous* glory **when it is working** because that is needed especially in the disconcerted rules of oppression. They get upset when you can think for yourself and do not follow their rules which were put here for you to continually falter with them and remain in an unworthy enviable position. But a people of clarity and free mind will speak of their acknowledgement to Source apart from the conquering efforts of any; and remain liberated in the same way to see their own light- divinity.

It is not wise or holy to project intransigence and arrogance in seeing other religious zealousness.

But regardless of the fact persist with your own godliness. It is extremely important that you do not become of missionary ineptitude and attitude. That is the **respect**- needed. They are going to let you do yours while they do theirs and reside peacefully. *That is the only way to keep unity of all human beings and remain in the graces of the Trinity.*

The weakness is being subjected to or seeking to combine a purpose of taking advantage of such an opportunity to control any group of people. *Those who are strong wish for everyone to have and remain with strength that is uninhibited in having their path cleared to* **OUR MASTER CREATOR**. That is the approach of being and in being to the rudiments of courteousness to all living creatures; and the down right **freedom** of others in being spiritual. That is the conduit we all must have for each other and her or his own astute spiritual practice.

We have to stay conscious of poison being put on the spiritual plate. That is to say do your own research of and on your own affinities of eschatology and *spirit*. This will leave you further away from being conquered. Then the oppressor is going to try and change or will change or has already changed the names of some of our great deities along with other things to emit confusion to not see the respect within the same fundamental truth while conversely hoping and managing to cause division; that will permit subterfuge.

This will lead to a wretched class of antagonism to allow conquest; and to promulgate a system that will keep an abject eminence. **That has been going on for a very very long time and nastiness has been chosen specifically for your people**. We can not consent or sanction a people to change what we know of *spirit* and put chains on our immanence. That makes it accessible for them to inculcate our chief aims of sustaining who we are; and preeminently we are to remain as a people and a network of autonomy. But when they take away our goddesses and gods it remains nothing left except to issue an appellation of subservience.

But if you know your Goddess and gods then you know how to call them. When you want to learn something about me and do have respect for that perspective; then you shall speak from us to us in and how it has been told to you. We lose power or the *electricity goes out* when we do not speak the way of the Ancestors; or someone tells us to speak differently to reach our pinnacle. That is compromising our *spirit*. The **Afrikan** knows it is something in vibration and the word, the drum too. You should not eschew those things which have significance that hit you in the heart and the right place. That is the magnitude that is not replaced by a defective interpretation. This is encompassing of properly adhesive linguistics and pronunciation of **our** people to also encircle what is written repeatedly in an effort to do what you or I and we want; and to have freedom. That will become your love and will allow you to further yourself in the personal aspect of prayer that is best to you; and only if not injurious to anybody. That and those actions have to become righteous and not just concerning the movement of the body but do apply mentally and spiritually too. People do not answer *when you call them out of their name* or mispronounce their name and the spirits apply to the same methods.

They deserve more **respect and recognition**. This insurmountably concerns your deceased grandfather to the consanguineous elder we all have in common to the deified women and men who have made our culture and *paved the way*. You can not continue existence of being without spirit. Therefore clearly it is how you act with righteousness to the universe, along with how you pray and survive, and how you have chosen to ritualize your heritage with ornamentation. That is beyond paramount to make sure you do not have attack and bakra invasion.

The *power* of being here in life with everything it entails is with having appreciation and love and reflection of us. It is clear to everyone that everything is not the same from cell to **soul**. We have different personalities and differentiated souls, each has a journey to get to, truthfully we are going to unite at a later time with the same deity of nameless and endless names. We are infinite in who we are but our freedom to express it is congruous with the humanity of being **truly** a human being and nation. This means our expressions and our habits are seen in the resonance of tradition; and are to have observation not critique. Each person needs their own workout and diet and personality.

We take from one another by the mode and landscape of sharing; but what we concede to integrate is our own personal certitude. I can choose to stick with a religious doctrine but my way of doing things is always and still my own.

WHAT YOU have IS NOTHING WITHOUT YOUR OWN DIETY

EETA

It is not at all whatsoever any need when knowing the fundamental purpose for anyone to have to take steps backwards or away from your goal when you are going forward. That means even when taking a break from some sort of endeavor you are still inching and taking the minutest steps even if just mental by keeping that agenda on your mind but not focusing your full amount of energy. We have come to the subject of acuity and truth withstanding intellectual freedom. When you have prayed right and **the soul is free** it is appropriate now to facilitate the mind. This is an easy progression after handling goddesses and gods of our very own spiritual practice to converge and traverse with what is one's own mental **territory**. This is your domain and no one must intrude (without your planned consent) or infringe on your thoughts. **That which is the level of your** *spirit- mind*. We need to keep everything ours; both in the culmination of education and with every quality of our progression.

They can not keep us from learning the right figures and information. Then also they can not guide us in giving our own gratuitous compensation to the **Afrikan** predecessors; or of partaking from our own conscientious way. It is not in their best interest to liberate **our** people and give us power. That is our **heritage**. That is why we need to magnify the components of thought and what contains thought, which is with speech and the next which is with spirit, as justly ours= in never having to appease a lower people with their mistakes in the exchange of our sophistication and erudition. We can build everything we need for every angle of the nation and from culture with **our**selves; and without the help of others. You can not free the mind without a *freed spirit* or the spirit freed.

That means some of us must get out of indoctrination on a mental and spiritual level and from such cultural standpoints also; to patch holes in the harmful vacuums. But while those who have broken away in achieving moving forward towards the pedestal must too pick up drowning passengers along the way we still hope that you do not lose your last breath or suffocate in helping those who do not want to paddle to the shores of **our** greatness efforts pulling down your weight and not *banishing insanity*. Their time, which we hope is soon, is not decided by us but from Source to reach her or his own realization. That may also mean to allow them the peace and space along with the freedom to return to a more holistic mindset; but try to get them to see things the right way. **But do not fall off the boat or lose your sanity for someone who wants to continue drowning**. We can not conjure visibility or evident hardship with the scheme of being deceptively veiled as equality for those who can not see the oppression in the midst of their life (also using terms of multiculturalism and crap like color does not matter for deception).

Our people can also unveil **a new** culture by the beautification and melting of the unending diversity upon the many strands we hold and have given to the world. But that still requires effort with learning and of the research to witness the similarities that have made and continue to make us greater. We need to make everything fresh and novel from doctrines of eschatology to thoughts of beauty; to have **our** focus on a global importance to reach such tangible and intangible matters. There are some of us who recast the restraining devices of bakra culture unknowingly and often exceeding the exertions of the oppressor. It is not hard to live in an **Afrikan** or holistic culture when you love it, with full knowledge of the meanings and intricacies. *We are using intangible matters into tangible practice- livelihood.*

But we have to attach the historical data with the objective truth, in telling **our** story. That will complement **our** superb heritage and immaculate ascension. Then we do not let people change the story. We can not get to where we are supposed to rule and have rulership of everything in the totality of our existence just to topple easily. We have always desired to know the full truth even when it shines badly because the lessons of plummeting are less prominent than the lessons of rising; and for that reason it is to incite us not to fall again. It is superlative to know truth and the accuracy that is for such; and in the confidence of your credence to battle the oppressor and falsehoods.

It is a blast of heresy and a call for war in *teaching falsehood* to **our** children. But we are a spiritual people and not belligerent. They, referring to anyone, may need to learn something and may have made a mistake and have need for an effort of correction to take forward to their people. But even still we do not want for them to feel more of what they should in a mishandled arrogance repeatedly taught and mis-termed as education (who they are needs pinpointing to break away from false proclamations construed as facts) instilling an unworthy smugness for these people based on assumptions is a disease of complacency fermented with haughtiness. But that does not mean that you should not or can not but must attack with **your tongue** to defend yourself; while defining yourself and your nation. The proverbial consequences of untreated sickness can result in death. This death is worst when you still have breath in your lungs and walk around everyday seeing it. **That happens every time we do not support or uphold the candor of information we hold as truth from the research and dedication of our very own** in the affairs of our legitimacy. That is in and of our **Afrikan** research while we have others who need and are intently listening.

They love to see when you do not demur or protest their ridiculous inaccuracies to permit these bakra selfishly to keep telling lies; while your being does not have the pride and **knowing** to suppress their foolishness. I mean really fuck them! We can get very demonstrative and appositely stay unflappable and contagious; while not backing away from the truth in **our** points. It is a way. That comes from our *spiritual existence.* But it is definitely still **our** intrinsic accountability to teach what needs taught.

Why do we have to have permission or have to ask to change anything, change your child's curriculum for yourself, even if you still send them to public schools for the child is to know the truth; and that the real learning is at home. It has been too much time wasted in not telling truth. But we will not sit down to rebuild/stand up later. That gloom of deprogramming adolescents in repairing leaks for the cultivation of our younger minds is terminated and absolved. That it has remained in this society is abhorred; and this is from the coercion of a brutally calculated oppression is also unacceptable, and from us not showing enough care for **our** uplifted children. These are **ours** because we have made them in the womb and with spirit and that which they are belongs to us; as defended within the nation until the last one of us is extinct. They are our souls and heritage and we do not falter to *get along;* because we want more than that. When we stagger and shift to appease others and their ignorance (not from our own considerations) it is pernicious. **They do not remotely offer any validation** to us *so get with* the program.

We hope you can see that we need this love from everyone. It is insignificant and without hope when we do not stand together. But standing still to is to get discarded is worthless too. We must move frontward and not sit for the dictation of unheralded tyrannical mischief given by bakra and therefore move with ourselves coalescing to become an excelled people.

We have to reverberate truth to **our** precious children. They have to see us as **their** examples of queen- pharaohs and kings. They have to grasp our faults to know they can have some too; but that we overcome them. Then administering that posture in our daily lives and that the same is expected from them. But they have to see us as the elevators of who it is that we are and to know that we are leading them precisely to who they will become; by standing up for the dignity of **our** standards of *living* and living in our fortitude. Your children should respect you once you unite all of the cultural and needed truth of being a goddess or god in waking up everyday. That is being in the appropriate manner of the nation and being mighty with **our** sagacious verity, which is power. We can and shall win if we lose indoctrination and take all measures for restitution.

OUR SPIRITS AND SOULS
FIGHT TOGETHER WHEN OUR
MINDS ARE TOGETHER on
ONE CONQUEST PRESSING TO
STAND MUCH STRONGER THAN
WHAT POSES TO REPRESS US

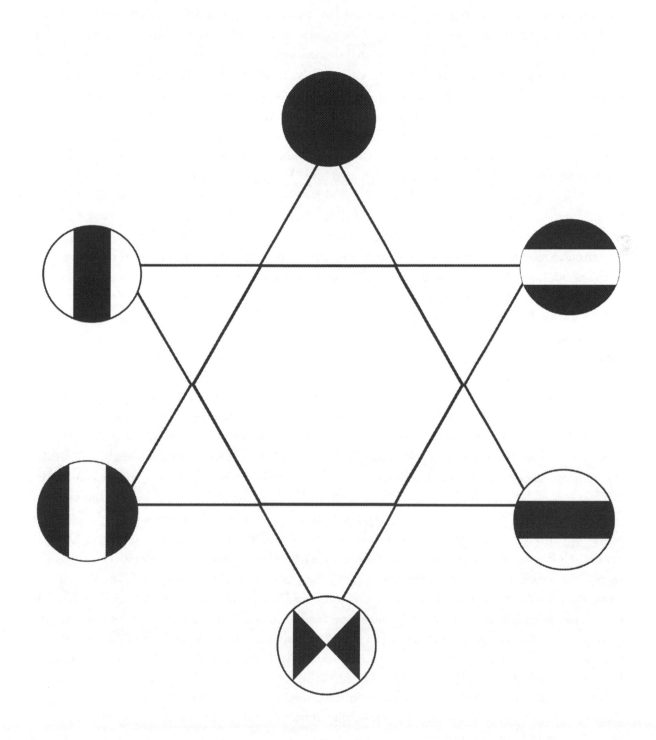

27

This is and was a very long and important chapter in my life. It was made into its own manuscript. The thesis was putting a chronological spiritual guideline in helping to deliberate to have a function in procedure; to the possible true finding of a right partner. Then from there and of itself to continue growing as an individual first; and later matriculating that to family. But difficult as it seems it is really so simple. It becomes complicated by and of; of peremptory emotions with human interactions and self. First is to find your spiritual and personal destination and next is to expand that growth from being however you have chosen to journey; either solely. . . or that in need of creating a family. That we need more **Afrikan** families is of desirable and of dire significance and weight. This is a mindset of conquering and of expanding and as so not directly reflecting the ethnicity of the person later that one may choose . . . but as long as the pedagogy and erudition and spirituality are of genuineness to our people. That which shall entail the psychological and communal attitude of our **Afrikan** family towards the *robust building* of what is considered love. The pride to further the nation. We need to get to places we have been before; but have somehow neglectfully allowed the bakra outside mind fucking garbage ungraciously to have changed **our** beautiful pathway. You and me have to learn strategy and guides for community oneness; solidified in collective strength. Then we next have to effectively exhibit patience from the relevance and truth of these lessons; and show what that is one day to the public, and the entire world, what one must do to **see you**. That will get you to the exemplary foundation of having someone; and of to treat yourself.

This is of first treating yourself to a relationship which is beginning first with yourself. This relationship is a vision seen as your thankful blessing from higher to lower marvels and a forthright concept. That is why this was accompanied with a picture. We do not want any confusion. That is what intruders have misaligned with sour internecine concepts which grotesquely have entered our spectrum and is being used to *this very day* to disable our loving community and nation. Everyone does not need to examine this chapter in relation to relationships. Some people can function by and large within their own sanctuary; and being sometimes to think of having a higher mission with acts of independently climbing, to a greater height in knowing all of themselves, spiritually holistic of themselves without attachment. That is having a fondness of the oneness of being alone **ALL-n-ONE**. You have to spend a lot of time with elders and of truthfully decoding your experiences and also too of deep meditation <u>to do what you got to do</u> to find that real answer. You have to give people their peace; but this also more importantly is to require for us and you to have a mutual respect for each gender. That is we need to know that only one person (the Blak Woman) is the closest entity or godly representation of what is beyond the stars and sky; and to treat each and every melanated conscious woman that way. A Goddess has given birth to all gods and <u>that will never change</u>. We have to protect our women from all wrongdoing of trespass and from lustful stares and also brainwashing and disrespectful tones to sexual lowliness and a gutter mentality and that which leads to dire bottomless programmed self-esteem and inadequate recognition with inaccurate portrayals of who is the neck from and to **OUR MASTER CREATOR,** connecting and giving us heaven. This we can do if we uplift *her* and each other towards ascension in the direction reemerging once again as godly beings. The opposite sexes must cooperate with each other as friends and a community to keep the collective going; in the incisive direction.

Umina Saba Nubian

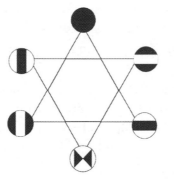

This originally was the Kemetic Star of Creation. But when respective to love it is the Sephedet- KMI Star. These axioms are the guidelines of the six points of the star which represent female and male unity prior, after, and during a relationship. That is the growing of both polarities are in union for conversation/fecundity/happiness/interlocking need/health/nourishment/and truth.

The upward triangle is the macrocosm; and is a must in being completed. The downward triangle is the microcosm and we must have the preliminary and primary toils of both to get to a level of love. These are those requirements which are necessitated to have resourcefully higher moments. They will encompass and incorporate **to rise within** and to also intermingle and take with appositely; to have decently chosen an individual partner.

The macroism is how the self will relate to community and family and return to self. This can not and will never overshadow the continued and lifelong work of personal development. She or he has destination with Source. You have to effortlessly decide, seeking judgment at a later time, to live wisely.

The point we will get to later is when you have found love with self and have inclined to enhance that with another. It takes many experiences and conclusions and resources in arriving to being at one and suffused to our Source, inclusive/countless/exclusive reality, the awe of truth. The life you lead to find self is also to gather the privilege inbeing with the Ancestors **and earn** *earning* **the receptive homeland beyond human phenomena**. This is the altruism and teamwork one needs from our community and nation to press forward inevitably/faithfully.

That is to get to Source by a way of utilizing more than just meditation. We live on earth with something better and greater *in mind*. But we must get to that initial progress. This we are going to step forward with by making love, this is not intercourse, rather how we relate and interact and love with community. Well making love to us (not from misconstrued sensual pleasure) is the *making love* by and from any interaction that can brighten the day of others.

You have to have peace and serenity in Source and of yourself in everyday living. We live in the truth and hotep of the moment. That includes nature and the animals and our spirits. That thus creates unity in the universe and the galaxy and to the appending next step. But we are not finished where we are now.

A person has to have the skills to coalesce with community. You should feel the love from your spiritual family and community; to help shape/mold/ sculpt your progression as a human being. This marvelous liking is the urge of affability and the craving of being affable; to get others around you involved in the community. She or he will transfigure success for the collective with or within themselves as the applicator and receiver.

But one aspect to clarify in making love is to give a smile to those as you pass them keeping their spirits high. A person has the ability to mingle positively with numerous people and personalities, by taking the good with the bad to learn more of yourself. We shall continue fusing making love with overcoming divisiveness; in also being in the search for the individual- in community. We were *not* put here alone. The best love is intangible and that is what you make with your soul and overall receptive demeanor. **You** have to interact with other people and refine that trait especially if you want a partner.

Well let us not move too quickly because we still have things to do sequentially in line before bringing a partner into the conversation. Those things will appear from a higher work after what you have done for the greater (exalting/beneficiary/sponsorship of the people around you and of the community), and of your network. You have to work *within us* before working with the opposite gender. But we are preparing you for that.

The biggest aspect of coming into yourself within the community is by just talking with **our** elders and other highly intelligent also spiritual people; to matriculate in life. This making love is the physical conduit of hugs, gestures, courtesy, speaking, morning- evening acknowledgements, smiles, proper handshakes, offering advice, applicably listening, taking advice, and forsaking callousness for the universe. It is *key* to not cause a rift nor an internecine ripple in the nation or our community to shut us down. That is no one should want to have something like that looked upon as one of their characteristic failings and imperfections. That is not to say a person has to stay best friends with everyone she or he may justly encounter; but look at all persons as a key to unlocking a door in the future. Everyone is a chalkboard and there are possibilities in learning from them. **We have something to give as purpose each moment we breathe with Source and our godly nature recognizes that; and from there excites a higher reality**. That which is returning to a whole. We do not need cruelty and spitefulness. But our saintly **Afrikan** intimacy is the process of making love and therefore not to have it is unwise; nonetheless sectarian and unintelligent.

This affection is our intimacy and our making love; for to not get it twisted again with mere procreating. *This has a physical prowess in the spiritual also within the oral of speaking things into realities and that is where we have more direction.* We speak of good things to one another and of each other and assist our own well- being by remaining positive. Those who are closest to you may have to scorn you sometimes but for the most part they should offer encouragement. They could also give you the final *thumbs up* when choosing a partner; after having gone as far as they could go in the completion of the work that was needed to uplift the embodiment which was that of shaping you. But also more important to making a verdict in becoming a mate; is selecting correctly the future for yourself. When you use this process of relating to community for getting to your personal goal of spirituality and holistic intervention; then that cultivation is an affirmation of symbiotic distinctiveness. You get from community **what you give to them.** This is the functioning of preparing you as a better person for the expansive spirit of someone later and then maybe for others, having our children. Those thoughts and conversations with community lead you to being a better person and potential parent with more to offer/give/have offered. That is an opulence of love in knowing who you are for the journey to take on *the mission*. But this higher form and level of community can have growth simply by choice; and is incipient with you.

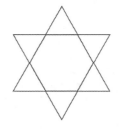

You have a clearer goal of yourself in of being one with the community and uniting with the many; then it is time to move forward to the beginning which is the end. We thought we were at the start with the first step but this **is the real true beginning.** The truest aspects of Source are unfathomable but we must get to a comprehensive accreditation, of knowing laws and complimentary opposites, for your ascension. Everyone should know that nothing matters but this accomplishment and crescendo; of an infinite requisite exchange. We are here to live with *the spirit* for Source and make our bright **soul** trigger information and experiences that shall pass the cessation of the body.

When you know there is nothing greater than the vitality of joining with Source then all points and tasks are in the perspective of a spiritually wholesome person. That is the goal we need from each member in our community. But when you *matter* to knowing existence **outside of matter then** you have gotten to where we all should get to; and to push forward keeping that realization in mind. This will keep you in not being selfish/illogical/irrational or *caught up* in matters that are of less than who you are, which is godly. It is not any way to understate this; or redundantly make this point. But each person is here to infinitely make her or his highest path way to Source; to answer for their own actions.

That which gave you life wants to see you **make more of life.** Then when you return forward to the duality and entity of that which is unsurpassed and is Source then one expertly regains truthfully towards your own truth; you will realize that there is nothing more than to have this actualization and meaning in life. That is because life **will not end for** you. Then the riddles and problems of existing are minimal; while the *supreme love of loves* is waiting and ubiquitously overwhelming.

Then you have nothing to beleaguer you except continuing on- in life. This is not to say problems will not rise in life but this makes everything explicable to that effect and allows that apprehension. You can move better with or without someone, and that is a choice; but knowing this makes way for that destination in your life. But if you choose to have a partner she or he has to also embark to the aforementioned level.

That is because you did not give she or he life and each person is here for their personal destiny. The opposite gender is meaningless unless you will to endeavor to bring oneself to such a function in being able to have this, the godly true effect of comprehension. That is why this is your chief acquisition and you must get to Source- everyday. It is an incapability to explain this light but when a person engages in it; **they know it** and nothing is known from our existence that is a greater feeling.

When getting there nothing **can compare and it is your destination**. Then you have become freed of being mortal. This happens as a return to something outside of science but of *living* and being human; you still have unending work to do here with the body and mind while remaining **Afrikan** and godly as part of the gift of your eternity. That is walking as a goddess or god still entails getting the job done on earth in the oneness of our being for a higher completeness with Source and the responsibility of the totalistic harmony. This personal growth is for forming and sustaining and breathing love. But when you know you can go further; this fear or burden surmises because finding yourself is really the only truth.

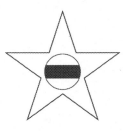

You have to have love of truth in carrying others to accessible means; for the growth of your communal and spiritual family, and personal endeavors. It is still one objective in life to do but that is incorporating others also in the love; that Source gave to us individually. But we are living to give to the many along the way because with yourself as with others we are spiritually evolving and nevertheless are here to give **our** gifts. It is time to return to earth and labor after being with Source and to work extensively harder- mentally. We are not saying everyone is a savior. But they are in their own way. We want to get to a point of learning and a recognition of ourselves so it spills over to the universe by constantly becoming brighter everyday. It is of the most true and cosmic law and forever assuredly known; that learning never stops until the final end.

But that is the mental sex of stimulating yourself- advancement. *This is another version of sex.* These heuristic adventures are enforced by cogitation or paying attention to nature/community/ interaction/spirits/reading and using all of those occurring familiarities to encapsulate unabated truth. But that is reestablished in the other points of the macroversion in sharing with others; while you still have to develop yourself and work to Source in working individually. *This is only the love of continued learning*. We are still cultivating self forward and onward before having your partner. We are going to get to the beauty of others but first we have to get to the apex and *beauty of our minds*. This is to keep building your full spirit and mentality to the land of an appropriate relationship, the other gender family and of our possibilities.

Your contribution in being an herbalist or mechanic or mortician or botanist or whatever; is to accumulate information to pass it on later. But what you have a passion for, being for yourself initially, will shine as a glimmer of magnetic truth for someone to discern later as very attractive. You <u>should know</u> that learning is being with Source undauntedly and exactly; but books that *cry out to* you are part of the path. This cyclical and constantly turning process of reading with your Source is in the unceasing effort of consuming more in this life. This is **that love** which is going to keep you abounding towards getting to a level which is you; growing more and even more to one being sustainably higher everyday. That undeniably is the better involvement of your mission.

The downward triangle starts at a high point of mental love and shared mentality and of being congruent with someone in of liking similar things or in the application of the same giving/sharing/bestowing in life. It is the microversion that deals mainly with self in relation to opposite gender and maybe one day having a family. But that and all things must start with the mental, which resides in the heart. You have to know how to advance with compromise in your relationship in having a *true knowledge* of each other, bargain together and towards each other. You are here for their *mind*. When having children they should have a variety and plethora of knowledge to choose from by each parent having expanded and worked of their own accord; to make each person in the household that much greater of- people.

But what is important to you and your relationship is to find someone who is giving and subsequently going to match your plan/reality/ideology. That is to say that if you are on Blak power then you need someone else who is not mistrustful of the same thing and respectful of where your life may lead to propel you or give you a foundation upon that same issue. They will give to you as ways to motivate or continue forward and monitor your progress or of giving so that you have enough angles to complement; as life moves briskly. These compliments and treats or talent to offer can range from cooking to anthropology to the drum to proper business management to childrearing to sports exploitation, for everyone is to find their niche and return it to the center of the circle. The children are taught and do benefit most from the pride of seeing two people *on the same page*. That is in the case of Blak power. But that is also with any philosophy or subject type with an expert in every field of every family as a small piece of the puzzle of returning us forward again; together as a nation.

That is to say we need your expertise to not get withheld from being prosperous within an inhibiting shelter; for the reason that we need to know what you have learned as much as you need to know what we have learned, to share that beautiful reality together. But that may go into being more prominent with a partner as both are to have an exchange of something on the mental level; and a fondness of what exactly that is, being shared between each other. This is a reciprocal flowing mentality of a reality of having a smooth congruence and mindset. Differences and similarities promote attaining and sustaining the *best of mind* in each other. This respect of minds arriving together and becoming sinuous advances health of self and one another.

You have to have strength in being smart. That is knowing the person on a spiritual and intellectual plane and consolably also on a mental level. A person has to have enough in common with a partner to know where to pull from when the times get rough and mediate (possibly maybe even meditate) with a **floor plan** that is for and of each other to get *back on the trail*. People who have a goal stick together from having a formed mentality.

You should have in referring to mentality **similar diets**. You do not have to agree all of the time; only rather you have to love and respect the thought process and uniqueness of your partner's mind. Communication with reception and decoding what is actual (not that what is conjecture) essentially is paramount for it is vital to have that in overstanding; the bonding and appeasing with each others' statements/actions/intentions. But that mental continuity and love will keep things cooperative when it looks like things will fall apart; this we need as a nation.

We do not need the physical yet or that which is shared with two people *in the kitchen* or under the candle lights because this is a time to secure more of our copious mental love, still current, in this process. This comes from a long process of mentally knowing each other. You know that this is professing to take hold of not in a couple of months but of years with a minimum of close to one year before getting to *or seeking pleasure*; to another height. Nothing will happen that is too contriving as we think to withdraw from the temporarily forbidden act of this holistic pleasure. But let us have it secure in all that it is with a sacredness that we can hold certain and together to not have stolen the specialness of that precious pleasure from each other, if we are to know each other.

But we need to have a strong basis in what we are to each other. We keep in Source of our alignment to such a power as the seasons change; in knowing that change is the make- up and epitome of life. That will show as we keep growing; and that of righteously having an outlook and format with life and the responsibility of our joined mental command to each other. When that is clearly stated then **we are** provoking each other to do better. We have the unison of what one expects to receive and what one is expected to give; then we have amalgamated minds which focus on one lingering dually shared reality. You are living for each other. You have or shall have created balance and harmony by expressing what your partner should learn from you; later showing that same receptiveness in being a listening student to learn from them.

Your love to this individual should make you want to work for love and to give; and offer the respect in doing that. We do not need arguments because everybody is not going to observe things the same way. Arguments can or will or may happen. It comes down to liking someone on a personal level exceeding tangible matters. You want to have a spiritual righteousness with your partner from *a tried* love and a truth of the mentality within; compatibility will determine that. The physical process will wait and explode among the stars later. But it is more important right now to know when nothing else is there and that we are not as individuals exactly the same as **our** partner that we have for each something that exceeds the body, a love of spirit and mental sustainability.

Everyone is different and must stay that way because not one person is the same . . . which is a part of the unfathomable phenomena of being created with different bodies. We are not here to figure that part out but to make life better with intelligence and trust; also keen perceptibility in the reception of the **Afrikan** way. But in choosing someone to last you a lifetime; things have to merge/blend/intertwine to a considerable point to not cause too many bumps on the roadway. You want someone to have the intellectual thought of reaffirming your thoughts (in some degree) which are put into action. They love you because we love first from the aura between our ears and of winning the soul; then we shall make the meandering to the physical, returning cyclically to the spirit.

But we have more to do and safety first, before getting to gratification. When you can sustain with an individual in life for the long haul then that does truly- mean something. But when starting out you have to make sure that it is realistic and not jailed by too much emotion. Thinking with truth and love will grow profoundly great. We want to see things clearly and with a rational nature to *not play the fool* and to choose wisely, this is life. This is the lowest part of the star because it involves the veil of emotion and superficial content which can change in a minute.

You should want something more solid in your life with anyone or anything. But that has to have such authenticity in the basis of real love and reality. There are people who do not have or have not sought both of these in the formulation of *their relationship*. This only makes the world more confused and away from Source. Very sadly, they are looking for selfish needs and not what is good for them. They surely needed more instruction to have looked upon in to of oneself before having jumped into a relationship.

Well at this point, you and your partner can not do anything wrong and anything done by them brings a smile. The both of you might or are in a universe that is not charted by the galaxy or is improbable. *Your face shows approval to some unacceptable behavior and even unentertaining jokes are funny.* But when that much love and expectation (the way you want it) does not fall in place all of the time it can result in resentment.

That can turn inwards to scratching and arguments. The term scratching is used because you may keep picking onto something until it has peeled away causing you to bleed; and this is the immense pain of a false relationship. You may not have even figured it an obstruction in considering; and either of these effects just continue flowing until the pain it has caused you/your partner is unmasked but unnoticed; only afterwards **seeing it**. When it is time *to patch it up*; this could have already caused an infection beyond medical terms for merely death to heal. You may have caused too much drama and trauma accompanied with hurt to withstand in your life.

We can not hold people to do and continue as we want them. It is very incomprehensible (of the lower self) to fall in love; **when you should stand** up in love knowing who you are holy/wholly/fully complete with being in the *spirit* of that knowledge of your partner, not to succumb to something inadvertently time consuming. That is also very unbeneficial. When you *fall* you have to get back up to gather yourself before falling again. Then you might possibly not get up or *stay down* there with a little less self confidence and maybe even more trauma; obstructing your promise in life. We should really have some reality. The artwork has precedence in how it was formed and the beauty of the masterpiece is picking the right tools to form it, a spiritually reckoning procedure.

That is in the triangle of the macroversion and the microversion as to stay careful of emotion (as precaution). We want to **change** our situation. Those are goals for yourself. Those are goals for each other. They are the goals for the family and nation.

The emotion of *being in love* should not keep you from seeing the faults in a person or what she or he is as your partner. Our personal and national revolution is to only change what is bad; to not being maligned to foolhardiness but rather of being of a just life (without subtleties that are selfish to the collective mindset). But the situation of having these feelings and of having to change a person from who they really are; does not benefit anyone in having that change happen. The path of getting intransigently wrapped up in having this change for you and not them is having a relationship which makes a way of being exploited. That will not happen with our most important and highest point ● being of the *Star* and triangle having been secured with self, make sure to do that. You do not need any other when you have Source and maybe it is your destiny to remain single; and this is possibly the case. But hope to remain truthful in finding that search and to that being a personal decision.

But some clarification is needed when talking of what is good and not good for you in a relationship because this is not necessarily a fault of her or him; just maybe you need to find someone else who is more fitting to your changing mentality. Guidance from others is possibly needed but do not lie to yourself when you need a change from her or him as your mate in life, keeping you from being positive, but make the right decision which is not simply resting on emotion. People will grow and life can change with the relationship needing to end. That happens with existence but stay friends and supporters of each other. We have to use emotion as a greater benefit and for **our** greater good. We do need friendship as a nation and not trifling or paltry shortsightedness of mere past romanticism; in the whole directive of the nation.

You have to act venially and with practicality to each other whether in a relationship or not because we are a **good** spiritual people. You and this person may never see things together. We of the opposite gender might not ever formulate to see things from the female or male perspective (depending on which side you are) still that is not a disguise of a fallacy. It is just that we are of different genders and cultures but can work together when we have a larger spoonful of tolerance. But we need relationships of the opposite gender and you can not have it any other way so that we can have family; and so we can have our **Afrikan** nation. This is to conclude in regards of our point of warning to not want control and ownership of a person; for you are not Source on a grand scale. You bring Source to yourself and upon having the endeavors of continually getting there you can share that by choosing a partner. That act of bringing Source to another person among your heaven on earth is something very special only shared between two individuals. We have to use this feeling and emotion and sustenance in an advantageous way. This is how we love and hold one another. But you can love and hold one another in and of a different nature, we have finally gotten there.

This is a time of finding more love and learning. But in its proper usage. It is not any reason to go beyond a kiss at first or to rush into anything that is uncomfortable for your partner. We are leading and leaning towards destination; also having found that mental stimulation with the spiritual acuity/cohesiveness and unity and love from our partner to put that miraculous interdependence into action.

Then we have arrived the correct way to spiritually fulfilling our partner in the physical manner; and earned our pleasure, to heighten our spirituality.

It is not a rush to get involved in physical intimacy. We just want to make sure people in our nation take the proper steps before having that. Our love is scientific and immeasurable and it is nothing wrong with moving slowly. There are options of things happening instantaneously and love at first sight but you have to decide that for yourself. The universe has change and birth; fecundity over a period of time.

It does not and should not happen more quickly for lust to creep in cursorily; and ruin all you have worked for to have with this person, on a more intimate level. We love each other as our goddess or godliness is properly attuned to; due in the context of the **Afrikan** perspective. It is an art how of we love each other. It is more of an art of how we *lay with* each other. The heavens fall upon us because of our melanin and spirits. We do not make love for we are having worship.

We are to **have worship** with the opposite gender. Then properly when the steps we have taken have had that time to muster a physical godly representation of the universe merging the female/male energy to one another and of ourselves in an inexplicable force to make way Lawdhav**mer**cyWoooooah! This is beyond what some people even have in their imagination. But when you know the science of the Ancients you can get there. When you have witness to the kundalini; and appreciate our ancestral magic and method of the actualization then we have returned our physical by and once again to where it is now spiritual, all in one act.

This is going to take all the points of the star *that we have mentioned earlier*; as with everything is continually cycling and leading to a way of more things to learn. You are going to have to read more on it and know Source; and not get too emotionally involved with lust to downgrade the moment. You are going to have to learn what are each other's likes and to listen to each others body as a form of physical telepathy and make more to form a discussion afterwards; because a partner loves their woman/man who can reveal themselves candidly. It is going to take some time in getting to this high; but stay patient with each other. *You know a little patience goes a long way.* But both of you are going to have to do some work to work toward each other.

This is a physical reality that still exists on the mental and spiritual level. The same is with the intimacy of your partner. You see intimacy and sex were left separate. This is truly because you can have intimacy without sex like with a foot/back rub or with eye contact or with someone leaning on you to tell you their day. These are things we have to have and learn to appreciate from each other. This is to walk with your partner in performing a scared function. That which is also *having worship* can do the same thing. This type of worship can clean the system and cleanse ailments (physical emotional spiritual) raising our level to Source and the one you are sharing this love with today. We need such collective prosperity and sensual delight and healthful joy among **our** people. A happy person will make a happy community and a happy nation. This is just truth.

THE VIRTUOS STAR is THE CHRONOLOGY OF THE FOUNDATION OF RELATIONSHIP

 Love of Interacting and Regaining Self with Others

 Love of Source

 Love of Books- Learning

 Love of Shared Mentality

 Love of Unemotional Reality

 Love of the Act of Physical Ascension

The word usage by the bakra of b-lack or black or to have lacking in some quality is not appropriate; because that infinite gift of godliness in being Nubian (appropriately) or **Afrikan** is found among everyone else and everywhere on the planet. It is a proficient joy in being ourselves when referring to color to have this quality; and is also first found abundantly in the universe⬡cell⬡spine⬡matter⬡crucial specific regions⬡ of the brain; nevertheless an actual people. This undoubtedly makes us superior. We have always been superior and were here first as the refined godly beings of fruition in being of a masterful creation and evolution of **OUR MASTER CREATOR**; and to have this strongest trait among any of the other traits compared to all those who seek comparison, is substantially looked upon in our favor even if denied by some for they know or will know as they become engulfed in the darkness of positivity that this is the truth which is the Blak Light. The truest light of truth is not niggativity$ which has sadly taken up infamous amounts of our time in degrading ourselves. It is of finding a reality and truth of a global connection with other beings who have the same light and want to rise to the same apex of unity. We need the darkest dark to bond with the lighter shades of color in metamorphosis to a higher actuality. This we needed a hundred years ago and still do need at this moment. The same efforts of some of our people could have been focusing that greatness that we have on display each and every day with that same energy on institution building and educational and cultural legacy. That in due remains conclusively our finality which we are hoping to gather by joining forever in an upheaval of; and in the **Afrikan** spirit. It is almost unfathomably saddening to think one person or many persons have spent their entire life trying to spin or catch or shoot a ball rather than using that same melanin or Blak power of unlimited potential or a blessing from the gods, that which it is, to actualize something that is going to have a lasting affect on humanity. Then there are those who sell the art of destroying one another and posting lies for the sake of entertainment whether musically or by social media or theatrically for just getting a dollar; not knowing how many lives they have steered or turned in the direction of a wrongful way, tearing our eyes and ears and little ones and **our** brains and neighborhoods to a dooming situation. Things that we have such as socially livable expectations and musical entertainment having been based in death of one another is unheard of from the heritage and lineage and superiority which our legs stand on; and is ridiculous to have roots in being some of the most powerful people in the universe and act like sports and criminology are sectionalized of the epitomes as being **Afrikan**. We need to ask why is it with things that are so detrimental and continue to damage . . . then how is it that in an already damaged predicament we profusely keep finding joy. Question: who spends so much time watching television or on their phone to not really think about that. The only people who can raise their hands in joyful response is the enemy. It is never too late to begin what was begun by your and **our** predecessors; and to finish it with justification. Our unified light is to have a global communal outgrowth that will take all of us and everyone progressively forward to what has been ours, shining once again in the light. That is because it is for the cry of the Ancestors to remain heard; and is for us to recognize that purpose.

K= Kemetic

M= Maroon

I= Institute

The acronym used in the star encompasses what we (Itopians and the **Afrikan**) are; and everyone who is that of any bit of *ahkebulan* –melanated skin as to find their way and path to a <u>Truth.</u> Of course that has been here all along vastly awaiting for us to infuse a greatness that is a resurgent intellectual newly found resonance. We have to get our minds back and forward to greatness. This is **our** jewel for opening up once more awe- inspired to the light that is hidden in waiting for us to see it forward; with strength and love to a prosperity that we have to bring forth from and for one another. We traveled to the fours corners of the planet giving out truth. Now, that this has reflected in so many different ways and has spun in just as many directions IT IS TIME that we have to bring it all together.

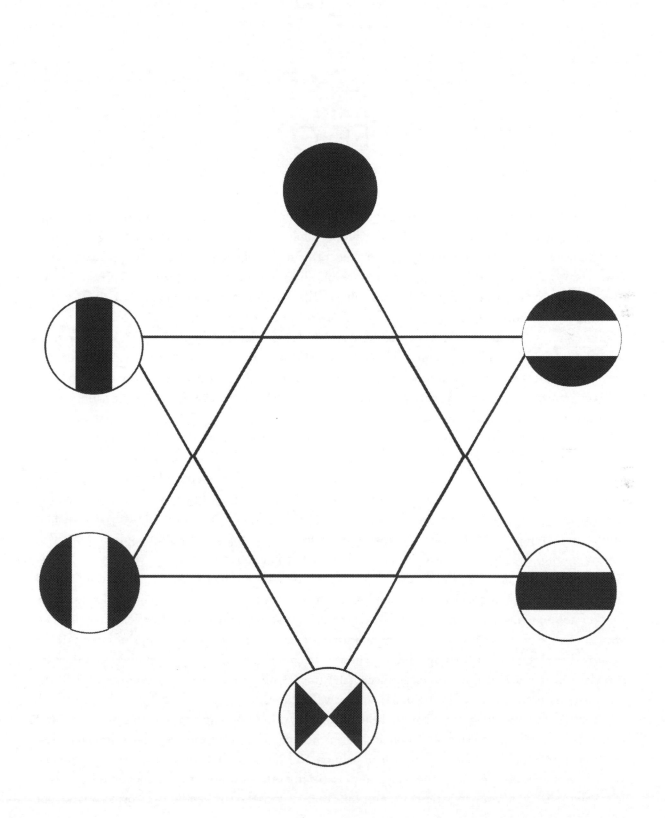

EEJO

A person should easily see that an oppressor using repression and control does not benefit the victim by making it easy for them to get fed the proper tools (good diet or spirit) including also such malignancies as to disenabling information and planting falsehoods. The enslaved Africans were given the worst food to keep their minds from revolution and some of us still will presently volunteer to eat that same garbage and give the same effect. There are certain foods needed for ritual to the spirits; and your body needs certain food for the *spirit*. These are not ersatz therapies for these are **our** customs; and we should not use other tonics to replace the purity of authenticity. This if we can help it or else loa will possibly get offended. A very powerful woman and smart woman at a conference once said that those who control food will measure to control the world. That is why what you put in your mouth, second to your thoughts and personality and mental hunger, is the most important decision you will make during the day.

How does your body operate other than nutrition, spirit is the answer, still it needs health to function and allow the mind to flow to its fullest capability. We must have and need to control our digestive responsibility while being aware of the intake and the mental aptitude of our people. This is so very important when some of **our** cognitive functions are bogged down by grease/non- alkaline food/meat/salt/overcooked/processed/hydrogenated/enriched which means destroyed/bleached fodder; and giving the effect your oppressor wants which is making you a walking grave. What you have to give up does not necessarily mean you have to become too strict to where you are not happy. But to accomplish many godly feats you have to concede something. Then also travail to reach and situate yourself to being much more happy with the outcome rather than that of the lowly wants that do not match the goal. But do not get *consumed* in making gourmet meals strictly to conciliate your savoring; or some ill-conceived disappointment from the perceived hardships of attempting a healthy diet along with achieving a healthy lifestyle **because** there are things in moderation that are superlatively wonderful and most clearly acceptable (mentioning to remark like having meat also salt) but with quality of the moderation and quantitative methods.

There are many alterations that are healthy and anything uncompromised from being natural is possibly healthy in the right form or cooked in the right way. That means pink- Himalayan salt and not nutritionally deficient white salt or salmon and not fried bottom eating catfish. But how you carry out the choice makes the matter appeasable in both the amount consumed and how often it is rationalized in your logistic consumption. That it is cooked properly and correctly and not over- indulged.

The *spirit* is meant to being in a light state and the heart not burdened; and while that reflects spiritual purity it also passes displaying analogously to the body. The lungs and heart have to have the non- viscous flow of blood and nutrients supporting the mental (to not have heart attacks or a state of cancerous cells) but stimulating your faculties in the physical realm. That is how we get the brain to function and the mind to rise, to **our** inconceivably incomparable heights, spiritually reaching far beyond to whom and where we must get you to levy. How do we get to that point where certain victuals keep us acting like goddesses and gods and less like animals. *The food is the strength of the result.*

You want to live like goddesses and gods then naturally you must have the discipline and a goal with that in mind, which befits conducive to your ascension. It goes along side having determination and persistent motivation too. But **that takes** profound character; and the same attributes that shall arrive from those efforts that will get you to a place worthy of our nation. The starting point is with the temperament of controlling your mouth. You control your mouth by the input of the decisions that go in to feeding it. That is also what you decide to put in your ears or the ears of someone else and is very much the same way also considered putting in the right food; if one chooses in the right things. The cluttered mind operating off and of an unhealthy nutrition shall live metaphorically leave her or his health behind and *unacceptably* say things while being grossly cluttered. That means to stay continually blessing yourself with *good spirit* and with that same energy you still have to have an awareness of your words to others to include a devotion to our community and nation. Then as we put forward better habits with eating with **our** body and soul and mind that which is naturally healthy while serving to a higher power your actions of having a cleaner life. But just getting to realize that; and by keeping in doing that is accentuating of a more pristine thought and focus, and of sharing our highest desired accumulation of deeds incorporated with the body/mind/soul along with our words and intuition.

We have to eat more groceries that hold water and that do not obstruct the flow of energy. The body was put here to corroborate the spirit, house it for a certain term, to test one in having discipline in treating a smaller temple before being in harmony with the larger temple of thoughts and returning to the Ancestors and **our** universe. We have **to rise** to the point of needing less trash and more refinement (like with fruits/grains and vegetables). It is simple logic that energy and vibration are not energetic when stuff is weighing a person down. We do not need foodstuffs but real food. Our bodies are mostly water so we have to return forward with eating food that is filled with health and nutrients and water. This we need to do before the transition and departure of going to reside with spirits in a heavenly state with going to a fluid state of *spirit- maturation.* Science around the world has proven that animal fat and animal proteins are causing a lot of illness within our community so we should eat them minimally and at least prepared in a healthy way. There are studies that show being vegetarian is the most proficient and efficient means to keep the body younger and not ill; but melanated with joyously basking in age and *not to grow old.* Well there are things I love too to eat and everybody has weaknesses when talking about food but enjoy them moderately because living longer is worth more than that small amount of time at the plate. I would rather have what I am proud of staring at me in the mirror of time with reflecting a body and a clearer mind of my or **our** nature rather than a short-lived life of less treasures because of focusing on the taste of improper health. But instead having more and spiritually rising to commence the joy of holistic abundance. This is not in having a comparison of the physical stature of anyone else but an internal awakening instead; hopefully you will see the results of your own exercise and eating habits. But these small amounts of time people tend to worship as they chew are comforting and deadly without the dialogue or cognizance of the taste of their food being compared/measured with living toooo a longevity and having time with creating more memories with family just does not measure up really. That in the end shall go with how we are fed in getting to that risen heavenly level by an earthly consequence of what you eat everyday. Well if everyone has to die some day (said by so many of us) why not concern yourself with oral delight in the short term *rather* I would think shorting yourself of anything whether it is money or time or health should hopefully or is not something partaken voluntarily. It is choice that differentiates us from beasts and not using excuses or acting on negative emotion (stinginess gluttony lust greed) insisting on **our** higher level. That has truth in more than just food and still goes with the *eating* of **Afrikan** reflected art and reading materials; to what is actual cuisine which shall give us the provisions which are going to continue to make us a greater people.

Our bodies eat everything they are given, food and music and thoughts, equating to an individual being in hopes of living righteously with burgeoning those aforementioned prospects. We are not thinking like we should because we are not eating like we should with importance in dietary choice and of health and prosperity. Those equate to the body and mind and **soul**. We do not say the meat of our labor but *the fruits* of labor. The saying would allow us being in harmony and rhythm with the most of **OUR MASTER CREATOR** and with their natural creation in having mostly plant and grain-based diets; and also not *eating or listening* to the degrading soul bending music that **our** Ancestors would not even recognize, that too many of us are enjoying presently in such destitution. But we have to remain on topic of what our minds need from our body.

It is the same as being reawakened like the ever- loving sun does every morning to our planet to bring light to a new day and a brand new frontier to search outside and within like the uplifted operation of the pineal gland. We are here to apply heavenly interpretations in a small amount of time. The pineal gland is the source and gateway **within the body** of *our talent* to becoming immortal. But it also operates off the thoughts given to it; inclusive of meditation/culture/research/countenance/ reading/generosity and of food certainly and daily. Food certainly that was meant for us to eat to help us to get to that godliness of everyday. That we should liken to being in tune with **our** own qualities and higher spirit.

We are the people of a higher sphere. Your nutrients should have the balance of thought and not the sole inclination of taste that which you can engender to give to yourself for a better performance and fulfillment. That still means what you listen to in music to what you carelessly throw in the shopping cart. The step is buying something that does not have more than four ingredients on the back. You have to shop for what is going to feed the *spirit*. That which is soothing internally for the mind and organs (alchemy of your inner workings that vibrate with positive sound to heal the body) will become medicine and adept magic of harmony with physiological response. The choice in musicianship and the books that you keep devouring also are critical to elevate the aptitude of the **soul**. We are going to lead further with that but first we still need to talk of what sustenance to eat or food not to eat for the body because that is critical. The main esculents here are not to have rice, bread, sugar, and salt which are white. They have been altered; and what is altered is going to affect you and your balance of thinking. There are few exceptions which are white like certain breads and basmati and jasmine rice which have not been bleached to ensure death approaching slowly. The problem is how much sugar (white sugar mainly) and salt is needed for sweet to still taste sweet to you. People have an addiction of sweet and sugar has been proven as a drug causing addiction and salt surely too leading to death but never attributed to manufacturers or those setting unhealthy standards. Things without color are out to destroy each of us and walking around everyday. The worst assumption is to think what tastes good or is good for emotional comfort is a blessing. We know salt is a killer when used unethically and is used too often even in little amounts of food that do not need it. It is also nothing wrong with cheating once in a while if you have learned to earn and deserve it by maintaining your discipline; and not to fall ungraciously back into bad habits. We know *dammmmm* well that not anyone is perfect and nothing is wrong with that; but fasting and removing sediments from the blood and arteries and bones or cleansing out the intestines from unhealthiness and built up mucus is of great assistance in creating a habit of using that ancient technique of wisdom or monthly procedure for about three days. This is what we think you need to have for your well- being to achieve or attain more healthy choices which are will limit the cause of later uneasiness or dis ease.

Everything has color in nature that is positive and has balance; and is a sign of its harmonious nutritious proclivity. The exception is cauliflower and a few others. The foods you think are white are beige and have color to them. They are things like beans, mushrooms, eggs, rice, and flour that have a healthier alternative also in a more brown shade of color. You should not think there are only white angels or that white food tastes a little better and is better for your health; when that is for sure completely and accurately far from the truth obviously.

But this directly goes to the lesson of removing what is culturally oppressive and food is one of them. It has to deal with getting rid of the things which we are accustomed to and where we have been misled by the bastards oppressing us; to function from the changing of that culture and to returning the nation forward to our healthier routines. The brain operates from the body, by what you give it. A person has to experiment with their own body and search the workout regiment which will accustom best for them and then settle to become their own dietician; and of course continue with change when needed with also intacting the arising choice help of professionals/elders and family with truthfulness. But the mind also has to eat too and conduct itself from reading life- giving material. Then with this having been combined with the thought invoking art and symbols of **our** great people; and of music and cultural reform that will then begin spreading to enable us to proceed to the production of a better life on earth. We shall become unstoppably regenerative to escalate beyond any other sphere. That means thus having **immaculate health**. Everybody *is given a time* but we must live it to the fullest.

You have to take in energy that is positive for the body. That inseparably has to do with the thoughts you are being fed and the food you are putting in your mouth. What you absorb from your ears to your tongue and to your oculars will have drastic significance; positive or negative upon you. It is not natural to listen to songs of hate and walk outside a loving person. That unalterably has to rise with change and of not immersing in violence, disrespecting **our** women, glorifying the negative aspects of the hood which have taken so many of our men and *real* warriors, making them richer with devil promoted materialism, having the lowest level thought, generating more adolescent confusion, and putting silliness to a beat to coincide doing what your enemies want you to do which is to remain as a slave not changing the realities of your situation from the continuous mental reinforcement of a catchy tune with culturally mental retardation. Your body and mind should go through the same ritual everyday; of eating righteous and proper food to have righteous and cognitive functions.

That is not to say you **have to eat** the same thing everyday but variety is the spice of life and also everything; and anything is possible with the world- wide garden. **OUR MASTER CREATOR** has given us boundless unending mixtures of music/taste/combinations/recipes as are with opportunities shared with love and culture; to give consciously to everyone more perspective and interaction with each other. But we are mainly talking about the fruits and vegetables when talking about **our** actual food; because they are programmed by the resonant information from Anwu or Jua or Aten, fused with intellectual liberating vibration. That is the maintenance of the soul and with the truth and essence of primordial vigor. That is something we need to return forward to and harness correctly; industrially enhancing the pineal because the darkness gave to the light and light came from the darkness. We are cautious of everything whether food or intangible that will enter the body. The light is the seed in all of us to bring us renewal and better revealing thoughts; to retrieve what is benevolent with every breath.

THE FOOD YOU EAT is OF THE SUBSTANCE OF OUR DIRECT CHARACTER

EESAN

We have plenty of authors and speakers; and finding your niche is calculative for us to escalate with it being part of your mission. You have to have a desire to learn, unleash application too. It is truly as simple as putting your intuition with your experiences and continually learning while doing so; also with the need and of the research. *Those choices are of true erudition while also deciding on the best materials that you shall read to fortify propensity.* Those elements coalescing only create impact; to and of the **mindful summit** of substance. That is why people who are teaching should teach always and speak forever amenably from the heart of truth; and we should have rejoicing.

When you are reading a book and it speaks to you it is because it has *been sent to* you; and to possibly make your life better. That is the **truth of cause and effect to being a sheer attendant** in and of the lining of the universe. This is a catalyst when that book is dealing with something personal of your heritage and of being crucial to those many valuable possessions and of that critical cultural scientific truth; making one's day. Those persons who have conscientiously done the cumbersome and painstaking research deciphering information may need **our** progression; in and of one day. But also we should give them what they deserve; that of future loving praise and credit.

A person does not have to make a shrine to every person who has written a book or scripture that has an affect on you; but they should receive appellation. She or he or they have earned recognition. *Their acknowledgment is more fitting in the day of judgment and matters most with the deeds of her or his soul but we should help them in and along the way in singing their praise.* But also what matters is the author's opinions and full inclusion of truth in their work for our consideration of admiration. That is segueing the way to why the **Afrikan** fortification of our minds is completely needed and healthy with relevance to truth; in expanding the value of our home and mind, to greet the nation with aptness. We need honesty and *do solemnly welcome truthfulness* with accurate information. We can not live with a basis of lies as some others do because it is morose; and on a personal and spiritual level too. But we are favorably holding on to grasp that which we endlessly will never let go of; which is to **have reverence with** having goddesses and gods of our very own to protect us.

You know some of these authors and scientists and majestic spokespersons have transitioned, *the spiritual realm.* Your ultimate complement and appreciation to them is to tell others. That is definitely trying to further the truth in the sharing of life in that of passing information along to others where bakra may have tried to bury and with their evil. It is something others are might not aware of that you may hold and to concisely keep depositing cerebral matter back- returning forward to the community and nation. People love being heard and still remembered and this would complete the **errand.**

It may spark the quizzical brilliance in someone's mind that you may not know of; who could have heard it from some individual who heard it from you. *We have affects on people beyond our reach of knowing and perspective.* That is why we always must continue to do good. You learned something beneficial in a book **then next** tell somebody who wants to or *is willing to listen* to help inspire their greatness in **our** Afrikan nation. Then you or them can or will pass it on superfluously for those other great people to have communications to send their shockwaves to **our** nation; and just as important merely to a single individual or another person. But in scholastic measures it is nothing wrong with relaying a book; or that of any information from what you have learned.

It is more like a duty. We should encourage that more often. It is stumping as to why we do not look at it with the fervor of an assignment involving a shared level of importance of *showing the light* and of being proud of what others have done before us, with the dawn of **Afrikan** civilization. It is nothing wrong with being happy in learning the many things that can assist our community and nation.

But we do not want to question the diligence or valor of what you are reading; only the truth of the content in the book. There are plenty of meticulously working people telling lies. We are trying to defend against them. That is why we openly want to make sure that what we learn and teach has the validity and credence of **our** every reference to nation. We **need to take** such aims to gather and glean our time to plant greater sentient upcoming production.

We need energy in motion and a spirit to express such duties; with a supposition that rivals the *call of military defense.* Our real women and men should arise up. **There are open eyes and ears waiting in the next world or waiting already at our feet for the next word**. Those in the spiritual atmosphere, not born yet, are *clinging* to the hope of us initiating something that they may have to finish as their call of a duty or personal destiny. But all of us do need at times pointing in the right direction from our elders and Ancestors to indubitably not forget the galactic **Afrikan** mission.

They have to teach us; so we can teach **them**. A person can work all day using the wrong formula and never arrive at a solution or solve the math problem, reading the wrong books. But the worst parcel is to pave miserably with rubbish that is specious and usually unverified; scrutinizing those deductions as reliant. **We have to hold and secure and revere information**. Then keep learning more and more but to also not keep your mouth/enthusiasm/vehemence shut down with your vim for reading; and as to never roll over being stagnant. We need to correct the mishaps and beam only the truth; and encourage the progress of those who show the dedication of rejuvenation. When you learn something new and different from before then everyday greatly is a rebirth, and the untrammeled framework **we need.**

This is not speculation but the mental and internal achievement of you to keep you/community/ nation and us going- unfettered. We want to move with the itinerary of our merits and of the truths recognized, never altering truth, only to change as the time suitably corresponds to and for **our** nation stretching forth to the universe. That means if we discover something greater or expanding on a previously known truth then we must revise the books and update **our** learning. Everything has to have practical efforts. We want to keep pushing truth in rectifying mistakes from the beguiling presence of *any manipulative oppressors*; to **our determining of** what we need in addition and revision from the work of your and our academic discoveries. This is how *you refresh* and review the old and give it new seeds. But new information is uncovered daily by the minute in our global **Afrikan** lineage and history. Our investigation of heritage and truth needs barriers away from propagandistic encroachment and it will take so much more sweat to get us there. Our exertion and strength is of leading the splendid truth meaningfully to where it belongs; in **our** hands.

When you can see things from the eyes and minds of your own being and our own people, truth becomes panoramic. That rises in being with as many reliable and intelligent people as possible to take along with the dutiful chore. This is with a conscious aspect in leading with the truth first which makes sermons overflowing with facts and those facts filled with sustenance. That will lead to brighter truths. This will lead us from the right supply to a correct finalization.

People who do not share our antiquity/history/credence to objectively debate our studiousness must **take a backseat** to our preeminence and learn from our culturally correct ideology. That is to say we want others **to respect scholarly** what is we know they cannot deny, our truth. That is why we are going to uphold and keep our supremacy as truth and our truth as supreme. But **we can** do that positively as the **Afrikan** for the reason that our exploits are greater than any other.

But if you are not comfortable and debased in seeing truth in our way; then change your ways. We are here as the concord of spiritual and intellectual prominence. But we learn best when the path is laid out with our foundation and with the terms of **our** resonance; in our heritage and culture. We indispensably must have the correct information and to say things in our way, **we have to say it in our way**. The learning and teachings for anyone should vibrate with pedagogical relevance as long as it has truth and the food of reality. Then that utilization is worth it; to have an ongoing discussion of more base and intellect and culture.

We want to broaden with truth and move forward, all in the same motion. This is possible by acting with your part and research. But the key is having identification. You really need to study and read the right texts and take everything higher; and all of this to further us in our definition of ethos.

THE REVOLUTIONARY TRADITIONAL USAGE of VERBALIZATION AND WRITTEN CULTURE IS CRUCIAL TO DEFINITELY HOLDING OURSELVES UP ALONG THE WAY

EEWAA

We have so much power in the way we say things and how we say things everyday. But clearly we have to hold on to that. Why are our languages disappearing without fighting for them; they have the flow of rthymn and clicks instead of a dry and dead language from a diminutive northern people. They vibrate more importantly with the will and energizing veracity that we do of **OUR MASTER CREATOR**; and not with their uninspired tone. That does not help us evidently in how we relate to each other or to Source, our personal destination.

That has an effect on our learning and daily communication and relationships because we are not speaking with the power **of our power**. We need to say our deities and the names of our children; and of the names of the Ancestors the way they would say them. That is beyond ghetto culture and more like **Afrikan** heritage and culture. We should not take for granted that european nations changed the names of many of our places and deities, sometimes being the same thing, because they did not have that unwritten verbal resonance with their vibration. We have that! Clearly, and the beauty that is retained in the mouths of who we are is the quintessence of the forming of truth; and definitely of our beginning. The **Afrikan** of past and present and hopefully future are *a very philosophically weighty people*. We are again the beginners of culture and civilization so why change our ways.

That is of critical importance in the reference of the cognizance of our facts, noting to these recessives, when they ineptly have not improved upon them. Then maybe it is you who should not wait on them; and take our cultural explosion into your own hands. The bottom line to them is of making money and sewing their civil- less nations empirically while still not being a civilization; and trying to impose not the real truth but something distant from our grading criteria of the spiritual world and for the **Afrikan**. We aspire from a philosophy and intelligence that brings forth from an antiquity; that has *a weight of the world deep in the beginning of time*. Then with such being said why listen and bargain or assimilate to people who just got here. **Those same people who have gone around destroying the world**.

How can you look at people who bring destruction in a similar light as still those who would or will bring any type of positive enduring thought and substance. This my fellow woman and man is a confession that states it does not matter what it is they try and bring (bible quaran scientology) take heed cautiously because that was put here for a reason too. That is not to say that those overwhelming texts and books do not have a lot of truth; but put in the hands of evil with a forced gross representation of sensible misinterpretation, they are attempting to still cast invisible chains on your soul. We have to have those books rewritten by us, **inevitably**. We have to re- start our own way of doing things and get away to begin and start our own culture.

This is what we have been trying to do this whole book. It is to get away from slavery that we do not need; and see that it is still **here** and there and now. It is just sad to see; when your people prefer to repeat some of the most outstanding and greater parts of who we are in the tongue and vibration of the oppressor, not giving us our correct power. *This is an unlocked energy that we have in how things are said with a truth that is in* **our** *truest speech in having a tempest of waves which will reach the heart and pineal; also the mind.* You may not believe it but there is a nature of sound reflecting in vibration and a way of holding structure from the first conception of things to the last quanta; whether verbal/ mental/physical. This is our true power and how we give reverence in the auditory that we use; truly an essential when venerating our illustrious past with the possibilities that give us the capability to conspire-futuristically looking forward. No one should remain comfortable when you know you could do more or when knowing there is truly more; **you do not have to relinquish but keep improving everyday**, constantly evolving as a person as something is better awaiting self accomplishment to your uplift towards the formula of any of your relationships or avocation.

We need to excavate true speech. That is us bringing our Ancestors back forward to us and returning forward with the enlightened warriors; on the inside and outside in being by our side. But that is fomented incipiently in how we call them. That is a big thing they want to minimize; still nevertheless we have to *look pass the smoke* and arrive plainly to **our** beauty and truth. You have to ask why is it so important to them in that we speak in one of their ungodly (death loving) languages or in their way.

That is easy to answer because that is a tactic of taking away our culture. But if you do not appreciate it; you will not find a way to use it- **the power**. People make fun of some cinema and *the force* but we should know by now that it is there! Yes, and it is a conduit <u>that resides in more than our perceptive senses</u>. That which is and certainly will always remain a very real essence. This is in the spiritual realm containing speech/vibration/profoundness and aural echoes to re- love ourselves.

We have to give love to ourselves in how we talk to each other. This is truly **Afrikan** in truth. Our people should use an **Afrikan** mode when talking about or referring to an African or of the **Afrikan** queens and kings of that country. The great dynasties of Old Nubia to Moorish Spain to Ta- Merry and any Native American tribe which has roots in **our** culture. This origin of love will bring us to the pinnacle and truth.

They who thus exists knowing that all, every human being, having been created from us owes us more than the breath they breathe and particularly but more specifically the Blak equatorial or **Afrikan** woman. *They have learned from us and now want to change our truth and deposit some inferiority.* It does not matter how holy or which holy man from christianity to islam or of any religion has appeared it is still (close phonetically to steal) from the soiled tenets of wisdom that which is from our ancient wisdom and having been paraphrased from **our** oral accounts/papyrus/rock paintings. They are the result of us fertilizing the earth, with culture and wisdom from the **Afrikan**, to not give us the proper credit is an abomination of being **too liltingly pliable** to the conforms of multiculturalism and not holding ourselves true to all of the heights we deserve; for our children. We know that there is so much more in everything that we are than what they claim as bakra still seek to throw a tremendous amount of poison in our brains today. But everything that we are is forever at the heart of being great and of the beginning of all things in time and of in being **Afrikan,** for nothing was here prior to us being here. *Simply* we can not turn the cheek of intellect but we must fight back with wisdom and intelligence. That is what someone has been using as fodder with depending on us being nonchalant; and of eclipsing our gentle countenance. This is obvious with the proof in their keeping this as a device and weapon for oppression. This is murderous and with the plan of our submission; and of **our** culture. The crazy thing is that this is happening while goddesses and gods remain in an asinine intentionally dormant stupor; and this was and is still their goal in diverting us from being our truest selves. We must build a revolution for **our** people and not allow any blockade. That remains blasphemous also worth fighting for; but the only person to argue with and have anger towards is yourself, for you are who can change things.

We can start giving each other energy that we once had in our glory and golden era; by cultured speech. It is laziness to say that an African language is too hard or the names are too long; that shows your mental astuteness between chess and checkers. You have put on the shelf your brain and have buried your mind; and given victory to someone without walking out of the arena tailgate. But if you want something easy and do not want **our** resurrecting of the glorified past then go nap with the enemy, you are not welcomed here. Then stay in your corner but when you do recognize your faults our welcoming you back in returning is part of our glorious nature; but you are going to have to work for it. Then ask yourself if that is the answer and remedy, and it surely is, why not work now truly and towards such **for the progression**.

This may seem of minor consequence but it is of a major deliberation of enlivening our culture. You may not know because maybe you do not know how beautiful the native sounds are of some of our very fragrant **Afrikan** languages. They make you feel good when you say them. The spirits look at you better or the spirit of any transitioned family member looks greatly upon thee when you say their name correctly; and they shall return with earnest to your assistance. But we are not saying to use these languages in overtaking everything you say so people will not overstand you in your daily routine of conversation.

But make a way to use them. You can utilize Akan or Twi to say hi to someone and have awareness of how much better your day goes because you are giving reverence to your Ancestors in little ways, that which count most, until going forward all of the time practically with your automatic responses as it will make others see the pride as you merge the beautiful fabric of you and us into the overall culture. When someone looks at you funny laugh at their ignorance. But if that person is an **Afrikan** teach them of the importance and of the heritage that you know of; to brighten their day. That is of course do not force it on them but they should want to learn something. These are our circumstances that need upgrading.

We need to say the names of our warriors and queens also kings in their full verity and strength. It is good for our children to see that others admire what we respect and that we are going to still give full veneration to our heritage and pride, setting an undiscouraged example, for them to follow later which is also good for the **soul** of the **Afrikan** and our culture. We are here to make bigger footprints. When people say they do not get it tell them it is alright or that they do not have to; but *you keep saying it until they do* either to yourself or loudly regardless of their feelings. But let them know you are not going to sway in representing your heritage and culture to the fullest, always exclusively until it is given its proper recollection. It is a certain people that has not stopped attempting to cause terror and have power. It is our urgency and emergency of to greater enhance and acquire meaning that we move forward and should always attempt to further, overwhelmingly righteous in forthrightly becoming better. This nation and **our** solidified culture that we are to create and to have is not here for their distinguishing; but only to exemplify in being that our truth is going nowhere. This is our filialness and we are here to maintain our precedence/primacy/domain whether or not you or them or any destitute scum like it.

Deities	Places	People
Bisu not pigmy god or bes	Lepe Lsut not Karnak	Heru not horus
Yesu not jesus	MNPHR not memphis	Twa not pigmies or first people
NST not isis	Djahi not canaan or phonecia	Mer-enjehuti not manetho
Asa not osiris	Amoor Hypatia not alexandria	Luqman not aesop
Ausar not osiris	Mellee not mali	Amayna-hetaupa not amenhotep
Auset not isis	Lunet not denderah	Ahmose not amenis
Anpu not anubis	Olmeca not mexico	Merenptah Sitr not seti
Sutek not satan	Mescachebee not mississippi	Narmar is not menes
Nawao not indigenous	Bawan not aborigine peoples	Aha not menes
Khonsu not hercules	Senegambia not Senegal/Gambia	Nganga-Zumba not zumba
Neith or Nit not neit	Tanganyika not tanzania	Nganga Zumbi or Zumi not zumbi
Mu (mooh-mueh) not pangea	Nahua not central america	Tonga Siba not sirius b
Tshonga not natives Shonga not native	Iwn not cairo	T'Shaka the Warrior not shaka zulu
Ubast or Ubasti not bast	Tjenu not thinis	Mosa (mow shaw) not moses
Amexum not the americas	Abylon not america	Kesh or Ta-Seti not kush
Emme Ya not sirius c	Miruhk Ahkebulan not africa	Itopians not black people or folks
Sopdet Tolo not sirius a	Lake Tchad	Jamassi not yamasee
Pharoah Iya of **KMT** not queen	Abyssinia not Ethiopia	Purohene of **KMT** not pharoah
Tat or Djehuti not thoth	Waset not thebes	Abyssinia not Eritrea
Amun not amen	Hapi Ohemma not the nile	Khafre not chepren
Ammon (aw moan) not amen	Lene Lenape not Delaware	Khufu not cheops
Neptet not Nepthys	Mazu Karib not caribbean sea	Piye (pie yeey) not pianhki

There are too many names to encapsulate in the rendering of our use for them. This is just a start…But we can begin to mix them in our usage of english or any language of your choice because there are many other languages that have become part of everyday dialect (resume` chauffer soiree fiesta checkmate encore blitzing). Ramesu not rameses more appropriately Ramesu SetepenRa Meryamun The Great. He was the Great Ramesu the Second of just one of the many of our very own Afrikan cultures; comprising the greater dynasties of Kemetic Origin- Society.

He eclipsed alexander the brute who was not at all on his intellectual level who also was not great in any measure to the queens and kings he tried to imitate in attempting to steal the legacy of Afrikan expertise and enterprise; by allowing aristotle to pilfer/copy the hall of documents inexcusably not crediting the many theological academic houses from where he copied such magnificence which his people could never have done; nevertheless could have never have dreamed of having the ability of incorporating such meaning just plain lies of inequitable treachery having later falsely credited in an undeserving fashion to an undeserving ethnic group to have been told to have discovered.

Ramesu the Great is who we should call even greater in our everyday speech. Ramesu II is Great and deserved of an appellation not alexander II or the greek. HoremAhket not sphinx.

WE CAN and WILL BRING POWER TO THESE LOCALITIES AND SPIRITS. Search the Washitaw Afrikan Empire and of the true origin or ethnicity of the moundbuilders and rich Mansa Musa, there are many more so go do your research. Some of them would watch the sun rising to say horus rising where we get- horizon.

WE NEED TO keep OUR TONGUE AND VIBRATION

DISMAL SWAMP

When you do not progress or ascend you falter or wither away into living obscurity. You have to keep growing. People need a fire lit of want; and a desire to get to for life. But you have to move to reach something. The way to and of advancement is not a stand- still process. It is a mission and obligation to keep pressing, *which is life*. That is the means of learning and that consciousness is to consist of you trying to learn from the truth of everyday; and to make a person have a revelation or clasp **real elevation**.

That is by and from and with life- *in living*. It should become very relevant to do this in your life. You can place that learning in any category you want or of your profession or of merely anything that brings to the soul an enthusiasm; such as meditation/your partner/channeling, as long as it is furthering progression. A person should not waste mindless time on their phone the entire day; and what you choose to learn should tend to aspire elevation or already is very important. We may have to talk with your elders or listen to your heart in distinguishing what is trivial and what is research that will later reveal a fortune of information; had yet to discover until your promising day.

That which can make your life better should become consistent and deserves attention; and is an orchestration of love. You have to learn the difference between meaningful and truthful and important; and capable in finding what is momentous in and for your life. But do seek to find unknown and evocative facts, which may have contribution in being potent fortunes which may lead to an uprising in leading us to newer information, consider the nation. But do not make this too time- consuming. That is because we want you to not lose purpose to who you are and stay heedful of your family; and prescient for the collective.

Any relationship should not become stagnant. It should stay invigorating to the persons implicated on all levels (body mind soul); to express that with accomplishment and entice health and discipline. **But to clarify anything with your partner is not trivial merely just love**. A person should want all tasks and charges to serve her or him.

It is part of furtively gaining the experience and **the lesson**. When your children are around they have to see this love. It helps them know what they are looking for when it is time for them to have a family. Then besides that they have physical work, chores help with mental growth, to do in the home.

Then when doing their responsibilities and work in the home they should have demonstration of the importance and of the purpose of this task by you taking time in *showing the lesson*, followed by question and inquiry periods. That means they see your love and that you too pay attention to them daily. They may need to get more answers from the work and you may need to ask more questions of them to unremittingly help get them later to those answers. But they can also watch you do it (then try it themselves). They can still exhibit that comprehension and concentration from the requested task or errand. They get more by watching the learning process whether academic or spiritual and then the conductive explication; by those who should have taught them. This creates **the need** of partnership and of caring; and of affection. The balance is for those involved and evident for youth and adults. Your relationship with the opposite gender can follow the same criteria. We should learn from everyone and not just from those we have vested interests in; but it engineers in being that much more special when both are combined.

Your partner should continually learn from you. This can not get misconstrued in being one- sided. But the shining action of silence is part of learning too. It does not have to stay with the rigidity of people constantly debating among each other but change is part of Source; and is welcomed when it can blossom into an alternative which will make something better.

Each person should make themselves not stagnant. The workout you use to maintain being a healthy person should change every three or four months. You have to continue up- siding and being anew with the treatment and birth of the body. It is a continual growth and birth within our bodies; concerning from the cells to the muscles to the bones to the mind and to keep **them** impelled *on their feet* and attentive. You have to continually feed the pineal and *the mind*. That which is new in life is to focus on what you are going to bring to yourself, with each second and breath and day, within this holy opportunity of existence. That means more reading and human interactions/discussions/holistic and mature parties incorporating the materials that do not inhibit life. It is completely of a greater human quality to have fun but still remain alert in how you do that; and in what you intake in the process. I mean plain and simple you do not have to get drunk to where one will not recover for a month or eat so much that you can not move for a week for the **wrong food** *is worst than* to have not have had any food. Then while doing this you are still going to remain apprehensively wary of the music that is going to reach your ears, and of everything that is going to have result in your operating function.

A nation should not become stagnant. We have to thrive for ourselves but even more so in the critical efforts for the young people and the elders. They want to know *everything is alright* while having assurance that our system is true; along with being assured in being able to maintain and continue our elevated efforts and thoughts. The elders need this before they transition, for their concern is the children. Our system and efforts require **development**. The nation has to become morphogenetic and still evolving for the regeneration of future needs in the having of imagination/discrepancies/agglutination; and to encompass from these angles with the forethought of everything needed for all of the constituents to remain flourishing. You will have to meet the Ancestors and elders **some day** and we do not want to squander our lives away from that realization; because you may return again for life is an unending cycle. That is why we have to keep moving and bolstering **for everyone that is part of** our truth in standing truly unapologetic with the reality of being great for time and eternity. Thus doing so is also an unending cycle. It will also uplift and allow us to have the need and to have answers that constantly rebuild reformation from which is upon our evaluation; and for the nation to not allow going stagnant as our death.

We do not want to die until it is time. We want that as our decision and have to work with the beauty of Source until time ceases to exist to carry on correctly. There are other people out there who want to make decisions for us but we are brewing with an electrifying culture to make us as the sole/ soul controllers. When you get away from what we have worked for; or away from this culture which is **our** culture, it does not help you. She or he has become a part of the stagnation. The life within you can not have the *pinnacle love* of these aspirations without the Universe and us; and of you and culture. This discovery of the flow and truth is unstoppable. This is our objective to sprint the marathon, not getting tired, because we are going to persistently condition ourselves to overcome and extirpate any barrier and of all those obstacles keeping us from living to that answer of perpetuity.

WHEN YOU ARE ONE STEP BEHIND YOU are THREE STEPS OFF THE POINT TO TAKE AND THEN MUCH HARDER TO KEEP AMONG THE LEADERS

SAN BASILIO

We have to prioritize and rejuvenate to take needed time **with our children**, culture is a child of sacrifice for the future, having worship with your reflection will bring about the growth of family. It is an immediate and communal blessing *and responsibility* to have children. That is the offspring of family- community. But family distinguishes itself first because it is the accumulation of such prominence in of being of the community. The community is shaped from the inside growing outward starting with each family. We see the appeasement on other levels and want to apply them; to dispense and create dividends for our larger scope of people.

Our families will have immediate impact on the community and collective; and the universe. A person has to make an exchange of the greater with the thought of having to take love to its new heights. That is meaning to say **with family** that sacrifice is intrusive but reciprocal; and the product of its refinement is the **Afrikan** community, to later pass on to the nation. When it is pursued and purified and filtered then the family and the nation will have been *fine tuned* to return forward; with more being given to you. But you still have to give up something as a person for us to broaden towards the universe and destiny and truth inevitably; as with any initial endeavor we see really. That is because to have something greater with having additional growth with the will to continue vying forth lovingly shall take patience; and must focus on inexhaustible effort and time.

It is not as easy as it seems to have family and allocate being happy or to stay happy. But we have to have the family unabatedly after having gone through the process of attaining our reflective duality or *partner*. The first aspects of destruction in a nation start with a broken family or within a house. The key is that this is our ongoing achievement to have to and for our nation. But at **our present** time some of our families are in dire menace from lack of heritage. But we have to reform our culture and start the process from inception; for the **Afrikan** family is to not have this predicament again. That is everything we do from diet to family (sitting down as family) is going to need explanation and have to begin once again to create a new foundation.

That we shall continue being more, with not just being family, but with everyone in **our** family and still with teaching adolescents and those who are parents who will have new birth one day in being grandparents. You have to instill things for the beautiful faces of the babies that you will never see six generations down the line, or maybe in actually being one of them at some point later or in a resonant day. Who else and what better time is there to start other than now- today. It is unequivocally the undeniable truth that Source blesses and continually grants life to the righteous. That is **to an individual and to a family and to the nation**. We must rejoice in it everyday and advance with the *opportunity of* exchange by doing more while the *spirit* is being held in the body. Your precious life of *living* is meant for others; and for others to see and to learn from it.

That begins first appropriately with the children and the community. We know that an **Afrikan** people **as a natural people** will raise a child within a family or group which is a village that will teach others and all within it. Everyone grows something special in their garden and we must put it all together in a shared and communal enterprise; constituting the healthiest meal (education discipline axiology spirituality philology medicine cuisine) that will securely give to ourselves for the future. We know *home* is where love is but it is not just one house. It is the neighborhood that we live in and the people we go visit; and the interactions we have in the workplace/youth athletic events/museums also homes, who are our spiritual family.

It is a community and a nation. You can have your immediate family but still we need others like cousins and aunts who are extended psychologists along with *not being cooks*; rather our makers of **Afrikan** nutritional medicine also termed food. It is a family and a community and the nation that we want on these many adhesive levels. We do properly conceive to frequently reach the people, who we need most, for **our uplifting**. But the final and true learning ricochets at home.

Then we can solidify and cement our thoughts of expressions and culture; upon the unity of having you and a partner working as a team administrating the process of shaping the family and the future. Then we can purify and filter what comes from outside the confines of your house or your personal establishment, freeing from the hindrances of pollution that cause danger, for they might not have any awareness of this as children. That is to say choosing for them the right peers and making a decision as a positively solidified family of not being part of a disdained and non- cultural behavior. You and your partner make the final say with your children/philosophy/home. Then as a nation we can truthfully sustain and admire culture (**our** own and others) of all gathered people who relish in learning along with sharing; to trade such attitudes with us.

The breath of nation is family. We can not ascend with what is not taught at home. That is the process of shaping our diamonds from the *mines*/minds of our adolescents and from our parenting and cooperative exertion. It is time we gather our talents and peers; and our brightest thinking to lead to the reproachable light. We have to **live and die** for those around us; and for you and each other. We gather nourishment from community. That is how we teach and enhance our lifestyle for the inexorable step to further **our** principles.

OUR IMPETUS of
NATION IS FAMILY

MALUALA

We are going to not back down but rather instead stand up for our own. But at the same time hoping peacefully to illicit **our** spirituality. People have made much of teeming laws and virtues but an overlooked principle in righteousness to many is being polite. Politeness is something she or he needs in dealing with people from different spectrums- cultures. But to digress slightly in pointing out that part of spirituality is for us to remain true and **to our own** truth, to have and possess that for eternity. But we have to act with an etiquette also a décor sometimes not found in others; and for that to comprise the personality of the individual. That gives way to more profound conversations and respect/communication/talking volume/sharing/demureness and geniality. We are too beautiful to act otherwise unless defending ourselves (our subject of the matter).

We can hear and listen but we do not have to carry it with us. That is the lies and altered energy from someone else like the bakra and the malignant pursuance which one can take back from this illness is not needed to share with the community. There are some people who have spurious arguments and specious aims; and it is very inconsequential to let them have any comportment on **our** way of life. That is to say it is your choice or the choice of the individual to believe or let things affect you. It is your **duty** or for each and every person to have her or his control as life proceeds with certain reactions (acts speech thoughts). But do not give up what you stand for by permitting something or someone to press too hard on you because eventually that is submission.

But you have to know when to walk away and not entertain fanaticism. You *make the choice* when to defend the nation or when it is not urgent or life threatening. But you also have to have the ability to listen to truth. But do not give up if truth is not something you want to hear; and politely give everybody their chance. It is going to make you better. That is with any person or position of circumstances or relationship. It is your heart that is going to let you know when things are deceitful and untrustworthy or belligerent. But peace allows one to become still and remain in your **Afrikan-** controlled state. Then we accept and listen and move on without insult/confrontation/altercation. You can not allow things to keep you from your thoughts and *spirit*.

We can not let them or anybody change things for us. That is when people like to impose their belief and make others servile and intentionally confused. That is disastrous to **our** nation. This is inclusive of speech, how you say and refer to things, make cognitive relations with things, see yourself in comparison to the world also the galaxy, rationalize contributions of your heritage, see the significant magnitude of your culture, have the proper respectful perspective of the opposite gender, how to recognize/respect your elders, and what to eat to benefit the personal and collective body. These people will turn all of that around to *stay on top* and keep us bottom feeders and away from the truth of **our** wealth. This has already been done; and we will die attempting to revert it forward to its proper affluence and natural order. We are the Greatest People of Mu and Itopia spread to all corners of the world; and that has more significance than we figure sometimes at the present moment. We need to give more than what is enough to such matter that is in **our** admiration; and to not to is irreligious, but that is what affectingly we are going to have to change with culture.

You must speak in your and our way. That is with language and of spirituality for doing what you know is and that which is true (trust and faith not belief) always having a way of relying upon inside as it pertains to you. This is how we conduct ourselves in dealing with other people. We want to read and reap the harvest of our truth and preserve/shield/defend it in our most beautiful way; never backing away from oppression any time anyone attacks it. That is to say to act more like goddesses and gods in becoming one with the universe when making a choice for that instance in time by not catching a charge; rather showing what we have worked for from the inside, but to demonstrate our power here on the outside (cleverness astuteness with a cerebral *mind* in elevation of spiritual guardianship) to remain godly beings. That which is most proficient is being a guardian of **our** culture. But there are exceptions. That we hope will not require violence or physical military action; never forgetting to always retain the respect of your woman for she is the mystical fortress that has produced each and every one of us. They are the foundation and main contributors of everything we see, without doubt or question, meaning keep the luminary protected. But retain **our** beliefs without imposing on their weak lies or developed stratum by uplifting but not arrogantly bequeathing our superiority. It is plausible to at least mingle some proud facets of each others culture as long as it relates with truth and respectfulness with each other. We definitely are not going to take falsehood and lies to make someone happy which **has been going on too long and must stop.** People therefore should know and see a difference and arrange to get ready; for we are about to arrive with change- revolution. *It is only something which is good for our nation and our culture and so for with this we can not consider other feelings.* Those others who are in apocalyptic fear of retribution when the tables undoubtedly turn and who only want to have actual remorse when not having an upper hand in a terrible situation do not want to see this; but most did not consider having any **Afrikan** sympathy and of consolidating our feelings in the opprobrium of enslavement or of the distortions of religion and science. But they or anyone should and are going to have to finally recognize and realize that such an undiagnosed and distorted sickness for the last couple thousands of years is about to receive the medicine and elixir from the **Afrikan** to vanquish any such ignorance and nonsense; and of reclaiming the position of our natural place at- the top.

We must *have our hand in raising* a respectful garden in the future time. That is to say we can look towards the future with our new wisdom and can enhance on old methods left to us by *greater* human beings. We have more to carry forth with **our culture** and heritage. An individual must have the authority/guidance/influence on how they learn and say things. One must clearly have our alarm potentially sounded for demons that want to keep untrue gazes of education and arrogance; for certain aspects of these people are leaving nothing but falsehoods that they would have us to continually battle. We do not want to hear anyone compromise from real truth or turn away from reprimanding scholarship. Traitors or anyone like you or them can keep telling those lies to the imbecile stupid idiots who must like to hear such shit-filled reproach for entertainment. But do not show up **here with it**. But what one would hope to change and continue fostering with untruth will eventually **show up** at the doorstep of intellect for not a single person to deny with the forced integration of Source; and such a chore is not for us compellingly. Our goal is a race or competition between and within our own people.

They just need to know where everything has started and that is with us; and sometimes hold their tongue, remain in a childs place, to know where the unbending truth has always been in reverence to our **Afrikan** heritage and to have to truly respect to know that. Well any person who desires to have an outgoing communication with us should want to put words and vibrations in the best way possible for those who are listening; while at the same time showcasing the emerging affluence and respect of the education of their own culture. That is for recessives to simply not impede on the purpose of proper alignment in reducing the speaking of others in a digressive manner to barter with communication. Then we see not too much forgiveness is needed because we have acted like human beings in making those proud who **look down upon** us. They see that our ways are working mightier for the global collective.

OBSTACLES ARE NOT WHEN WE CONTINUE in OUR WAY OF HERITAGE Peace will continually stay, to appear within.

CHARACTERISTICS

self: actualization, finding purpose, living righteously, enhancing traits, filial respect, strengthening weaknesses, truthfully honest, giving forward

family: urging, motivation, affection, support, temperament, altruism, uplifting, fort

community: encouragement, tradition, intuitive, advice, rituals, validity, axis reassurance

nation: axiology, dignity, pedagogy, reflecting, increasingly potent, responsible, protection, breathtakingly pulsating

collective: affable, evident, vivifying, soothing, disciplined, laudatory, innovative, gratuitous

Appendix

I would suggest reading chapter 7 lastly.
I would suggest reading it chronologically first, before pairing them.

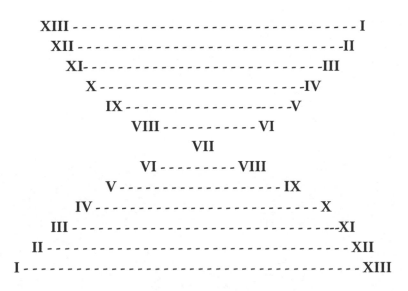

XIII - I
XII -II
XI- -III
X -IV
IX - - - - - - - - - - - - - - - - - -V
VIII - - - - - - - - - - - VI
VII
VI - - - - - - - - - VIII
V - - - - - - - - - - - - - - - - - - IX
IV - X
III -XI
II - XII
I - XIII

DNA

GLOSSARY

bakra} white people or european

watoto} Kemetic Society for children

Sunnum Bunnom} Kemetic Society for being with and of the greater good

loa} deity or Haitian spirit in Vadou

hotep} Kemetic Society for peace

having worship} The act of/to have spiritual intercourse in the physical realm for the

Afrikan

NTUNYEYE

I love that there is so much to love when there is self-growth and being independent and self-sufficient. **Onyam**(Trust me) (**ohn~own yawm**)

These are some phrases of wisdom:

- We form a chain or link, lasting forever, all women and men.
- The melanated potentially divine woman and superior man must recognize each other as limitless to recognize themselves.
- The Blak woman is the end of development, also the beginning.
- You think in assuming fact rather than to know and prove it.
- Diligence is a trait if you want it.
- A boy is to become a man but a Nubian Queen is a Blak Queen at birth.
- The world has an obligation to refine me; and I definitely have to better the world.
- You will never and never can become a man first, spiritually or mentally among others also scientifically, without the love of a woman.
- Well how can everybody change the world in someone else but not in theirselves; do not become hypocrisy.
- Wisdom is for our colorful collective and together with the galactic cooperation and tolerance we will also produce; to give more to the Afrikan nation.
- When usage of elemental and spiritual forces try thus adhering in resulting to a true manifestation of the aspiring girl or boy, becoming a leader with the holistic goal to embody a responsible handler of power, just flows naturally and is ancillary.
- The easy road will become hard while divinely the hard road will become easy.
- But we must continue or fall to the side.
- But you should not desire being average because truth for the average person is what she or he is satisfied to hear.
- But you should make way for love without giving away from responsibility.
- Source knows everything we do not know and all that we do know just on a higher level.
- Philosophies in life can differ in the personality of each individual.
- But people who want aimlessly need better stop; and attempt to realize if that is for them.
- One step is better than standing still.
- But those who learn their apparent lessons take recognition to apply them.
- Well to give and take without obligation is love.

- What is a need is what sustains life.
- The most important step is the beginning.
- But happiness does not exist in the external world but by such things that exist within us.
- But when you learn to debate rather than argue; then you have conquered a form of existence.
- What have you done with life today.
- But one shall continue on being without until accomplishing within; your mind.
- Your love should become and keep becoming and not wait until the final moment.
- We have to stay prescient and prepared; to enhance security and direction.
- But divine law is upheld by the righteous; not only in action but with thought.
- You must fight on having spirituality with the paramount aim of preservation.
- But when making special your strength do not forget your weaknesses.
- But the biggest of all shortcomings is to think to not have any faults.
- There are not any differences in legitimate reasons and excuses when the job is not done.
- Everything arrives to fruition and is in existence by love; and the way of you.
- Those who fortify theirselves and have discipline have the most power.
- Well darkness having been focused or is sometimes termed as meditation in proving fact can make the ambiguous clear.
- Your dreams are different realities.
- But any form of compulsion is a form of slavery.
- You do all that you can do to surmount the fear of not doing.
- But trying to find something for personal benefit in someone else is degrading because you are your perfect match.
- You should not overlook any circumstance to and for our nation.
- A certain people had us appreciate their insanity.
- But profound analysis with critical thinking is the restoration of time.
- You should leave what you love for service and return forward.
- But to drown overly in one thought is to cloud your vision.
- But sometimes to find the truth you have to discover a lie.
- You do not drown by falling into water; you drown by staying in it.
- They will try to get you to believe in anything and everything instead of finding the truth in something.
- You have to stay aware of everything outside that can affect inside.
- But perpetual change means evolution.
- Children will go hungry or learn good eating habits at my table.
- We have to have conscious consumption of our actions and food and spirits.
- But you must learn to work spiritually with body and mind which is not perfect for you to strive for perfection.
- Youth is a gift from heaven; and age profoundly consumed with growth is a work of art undoubtedly and with certainty.
- Empirical benchmarks of love are giving and letting go and sharing.
- The perfection of the womb is more than the house of the seed but the home of the first feelings of love, rhythm, thought, nutrition, and spirit.
- Well ignorance is not lack of intelligence but lack of knowledge.

- But as long as you have thought then you have limitless opportunity and chance.
- Truthfully I can not expect you to show any light until I myself have become a beacon; of an example.
- People get disease by their mentality.
- We must never lose truth to unify; and bringing forward again our ancestry and greatness as one.
- But people tend to love what they can not have and not appreciate what has been there all of the time.
- You never judge anyone from any such dislike of personal opinion; for you may have those traits in lesser degree.
- You can not achieve a higher level unless you practice at a high level.
- We should take heed to what can aspire and promote healthy soulful relationships and exchange.
- Real people are impressed by character and not money.
- Well I give honor and reverence and wisdom to those who honor me.
- When is it that neither opinion is right or wrong but both are needed; it is often.
- It is either a sign or crossroads in everything.
- It is just another form of Source so I can not fear it.
- Well emotions and feelings are good administrators and subordinates yet hopelessly bad masters.
- There are not any persons more important in life than an unborn child;
- accumulation of spirits revisited.
- We have to plant our own seeds.
- But some things can or will resonate as limitlessly continuing and not culminated; such is life.
- A good upbringing is another name for peace and bliss.
- You work today for tomorrow.
- But every thought or theology must become better anew; because you are here.
- It is sometimes for the future generations to give again to the elders who may return in another form to not finish the job but start the task for other people; for them to later solidify.
- Prophecy does not happen until you make it happen.
- You must return to the inner soul.
- The task ahead of you is never as great as the power within or inside of you.
- Whether or not you know it; truth is truth.
- The truth is true miracles happen everyday.
- Your truth is an ever evolving multi- faceted examination.
- A being is a conscious and spiritual individual.
- You should not allow or become mystified by your own mysticism; you are what is or what shall grow to your finest purified capability.
- But you can not do anything without the Ancestors.
- I walk alone because I am never alone.
- We should treat each being and existent with proper righteous protocol.
- But excellence is doing something uncommon in a common way.
- But happiness is not living with money but creating your own riches.

- I am a man serviceable to our and my community woman nation and will take the lead or keep up.
- Respect and service is the rent for the privilege of living.
- People have the right in always being loved; but not always to adhering to your opinion.
- When everybody becomes one with her or his divinity in the spiritually expressive singular; then everybody can become one whole.
- We have to stay humble.
- People have mishandled truth and some have mistaken power for greatness.
- Wrong is the opportunity to learn something.
- It is hard to think when you only think what you think.
- The pleasure of happiness lies in a power of extracting greatness with joy from common things.
- The real woman or man will take disadvantages and insurmountably arrive out advantageous; not bragging about it.
- It is distinguishable to one and of a different plane to praise having discipline; another to submit to it.
- You sometimes have to lose a part of yourself to become whole.
- People have to see the right while at the same time recognizing the wrong.
- When greatness is realized within then it can become an actuality of your potential and reality.
- You must have our church and your own congregation internally.

I would suggest reprinting or cutting out each and every one of them. This does not have to replace your ideology or oracle; but is a compliment to your regular. I would then take one or two of them, law of complimentary opposites, and have them as phrases of the week being that there are a total of 104 in having your weekly possibility of dual aspects for contemplation. You could put a different one on different sides of the door or opposite sides of the sink. It is hard to pull or maybe have the same pairings each year. But as long as they induce thought and give to introspection for accomplishment to help throughout your enlightened journey. These can help throughout the day. One can have a bowl of them at your desk just when needing to focus and reset your **Afrikan** mentality; when the circumstances get hectic and call you to get away. You could or may want to give them out in your office monthly. But the most important person is you (fixating the spiritual) and becoming whole. Finding you is up to yourself.

NOTES

COMMERCIAL BREAK

Urgent Urgent

We need to get some lies straight. The first sin is not having melanin. **Our** Most High never makes mistakes; humans go in the wrong direction like a bad child, looking to blame mishap and insecurity outside of the facet of truth and the internal mirror. Nothing is stronger than the ubiquitous ever-present unfathomable omnipotent incomprehensible power which always is and whilst undoubtedly is Source ↕∞↕ therefore nothing can exist which can rival something that has no match to keep you from your godly destination. People would like to blame or use an excuse of other little devils, without doubt all of that is within, but you can not have truth in Source within oneself if you believe something is out there to defeat it. We are here to return to **our** righteousness and have led and have to lead again correctly to the ordained righteous way. So when people go the wrong way turning towards the right way is a long road to go; just to get back to the point where you should not have left from in the beginning but instead to get there with humility. That is what happened with these lesser beings who left Africa and who genetically mutated and reformed into a retarded version of a human being to what we have in the present day. They may have been ostracized because of albinism or were sent on a journey and suddenly trapped in another northern regional ice storm or were looking to expand but never returned. But being that they have returned upset and disappointed and with a vengeance; and slick and conniving in terms of being unhealthy (physically/spiritually) is for certain overt in their disposition and away from the original loving mentality. The plight of not having light physically and mentally in a dark cold and brutally competitive region drained their bodies of the super-food called melanin. When you leave the misguided alone in a room without the beautiful proven ways of old then there is a torture that ferments into a sickness and death prevails as harmful retribution alas from not being corrected; not knowing truth or that of any other guidance. You see it as your way and the only right way. That is what happened with these people. But without spiritual foresight this has become utterly destructive and it is completely wrong, and globally detrimental. The inability to produce melanin or not having produced melanin; and being forced from the garden of eden outside of the homeland is a travesty. But the world should not have to pay for that physiological and psychological trauma. The sun is too powerful and can burn and hurt those not blessed externally with the universe; capsulated in one melanin cell. Yes, you would have to cover up with leaves and blame a snake and keep everybody from really looking at your external flaw. We are not going to talk about how it smells and is filled with disease and ages quickly. Those are scientific matters already proven. But the spiritual matter that was taken away is of the most abundant prominence, being that beatific melanin, and until you rise that Blak light on the inside you must know your place on the outside. Then get blessed of course by being led by those beings who have abundantly inherited it in their skin. We are here to not take any excuses or to have any prisoners in our constructive retribution of the light in bringing a new day. I along with the **Afrikan** simply say that my people are building and arriving to the day of a special inevitable nature of becoming soldiers or teachers (your choice), or both. We can not let these people get the job done of destroying the universe in an attempt to deplete from karmic happenstance what the rest of the living creatures in the universe has in this oh so rich blessing; and that which is with what they do not have in **our** melanin. You can not take everything away from us until we have nothing left except in maintaining ways that are incomprehensible albeit confused and being mentally coerced to retain existing without pride (of the beauty we have scientifically and historically and internally). You are upset at the universe and galaxy; and want to destroy everything in it for it is you who does not have the luxury of externally storing this blessing: melanin. That insecurity is unquestionably demonic. You want to preserve your flaw and have us pass it on consentingly as some uncertain good trait until the greater can not rise any higher than the lesser *the reason some would call you a devil*. But we are not going to digress to violence or hatred unless needed. Well then, we are going to start getting forward to the noble parameters from which we set and have had before in ancient times. Then also we are going to stop looking to the problem for the answer and then eradicate instead of pacifying the germ; and stop having the lies breathed upon totality that exists to the colorful Moorish Umoja. The oldest profession is mid-wifery and spiritual astrology. How are you going to take anything on your life's mission as being most important from a people who practice falsehood and also deconstruct facts. Then these people are going to hold deviously an arrogance of such disaster or calamity founded on the constant smothering of lies above your head as an inconspicuous reason for having then dictated what goes on around the world. These sorry people are going to take all of the indigenous portrayals of **OUR MASTER CREATOR** and falsify these images of God; *how low can such people stoop*. Then for them to say that this ungodly purpose or reason is to bleach our solar system, in a straight face, and turn all other people into the absurd is but having correct vision from their eyes of bequeathing their illegitimate way. They have made everyone look at imperialism and domination as being viewed as proper bakra insanity. But the trick is to cloak and keep everybody crazy so it does not seem irrational; as they savage to take all of the resources and money. Then even using movie style technology to make documents look old and vintage; to leave the hook in your mouth, holding your mental but from going so far with religious backing to condemn anyone having questions as if the ever loving God that we may know does not want us to learn constantly and embrace everything. But instead wait despairingly for answers out of the sky or for financially seeking demonic clergy. That is the greatest lie to never get answered which is to remain in ambiguity, to keep us from what we need in spirituality.

Negusa (Afrikan-American/Afrikan Male) and Njau (young bull) I want to talk directly to you in **our** quest to legitimately uphold and protect Ankh (the Blak Afrikan Nubian Woman) as **our** most truest dire responsibility. We can not idly stand to any defamation or disrespect that goes along her way. We can not encourage behavior at a young age or any age that is not befitting of a lady. These are things we have let other bakra lesser species take control of and rather dictate what is acceptable in our view of being worthy to **our** women, in their treatment, perception, esteem, health, status, and comfort. I know so many of **our** women still desire us. They have looked out for us since before we got off the ship. They were here to stand beside (not behind) us or provide family and true warriors the motivation to incite us against invasion. I know we can do better for them today until forever if each gender can grow and live up to their birthright truly.

I am not talking about the distorted views one sees on television. That is not what we are- either side. **Afrikan** women and **Afrikan** men are far greater than what they try and debase us with in *reality shows* and propaganda, nothing even resembling a true **Afrikan**. We have got to stop letting other people think for us. It is sad they want you to think of yourself in the perception they think of you. I want you to think about that for a minute and repeat it to yourself. Women have to start putting better limits on the box or different criteria for the fruit or more Nubian parameters befit of real men being rewarded of the most precious gift on Earth, outside of the breath of **OUR MASTER CREATOR**, then both genders rise wholeheartedly to change the world. If women want men to act like men then Ankh must become real women. Then only give the good stuff to scholars and warriors and not criminals. We as men would change for humanity and for the greater of ourselves quickly.

written by
NSahale M'Abiola

Printed in the United States
By Bookmasters